OAuth 2.0 Simplified

A guide to building OAuth 2.0 servers

Aaron Parecki

OAuth 2.0 Simplified

by Aaron Parecki

Copyright © 2021 by Aaron Parecki

Illustrations Copyright © 2021 by Okta, Inc.

OAuth Logo by Chris Messina

Published by Okta, Inc. 100 1st St 6th Floor, San Francisco, CA, 94105

While every precaution has been taken in the preparation of this book, the publisher and the author assume no responsibility for errors or omissions, or for damages resulting from the use of the information contained herein.

ISBN: 978-1-387-75151-8

21350.1546

Fourth Edition

Table of Contents

Preface vii

Acknowledgments viii

Background ix

Part I. OAuth 2.0 Clients

1. Getting Ready 15
   Creating an Application 15
   Redirect URLs and State 16
2. Accessing Data in an OAuth Server 19
   Create an Application 19
   Setting Up the Environment 22
   Authorization Request 24
   Obtaining an Access Token 25
   Making API Requests 27
3. Signing In with Google 29
   Create an Application 30
   Setting Up the Environment 31
   Authorization Request 32
   Getting an ID Token 34
   Verifying the User Info 36
4. Server-Side Apps 41
   Authorization Code Flow 42
   Example Flow 46

OAuth 2.0 Simplified

Possible Errors..49
Ｕser Experience and Security Considerations......................51

5. **Single-Page Apps**...53
   Authorization...54
   Example Flow 57
   Sample JavaScript Code...59
   Implicit Flow...61
   Security Considerations 62

6. **Mobile and Native Apps** 65
   Authorization...65
   Security Considerations 70

7. **Making Authenticated Requests** 71
   Refresh Tokens 73

Part II. Building an OAuth 2.0 Server

8. **Client Registration** 79
   Registering a New Application.......................................79
   The Client ID and Secret..83
   Deleting Applications and Revoking Secrets...................87

9. **Authorization**...89
   The Authorization Request 89
   Requiring User Login 93
   The Authorization Interface 95
   The Authorization Response 99
   Security Considerations 104

10. **Scope** 109
    Defining Scopes 110
    User Interface 112
    Checkboxes 115

11. **Redirect URLs** 121
    Registration...121
    Redirect URLs for Native Apps....................................123
    Validation..125

12. Access Tokens 127
Authorization Code Request 128
Password Grant 131
Client Credentials 132
Access Token Response 133
Self-Encoded Access Tokens 137
Access Token Lifetime 142
Refreshing Access Tokens 145

13. Listing Authorizations 149
Revoking Access 153

14. The Resource Server 155

15. OAuth for Native Apps 159
Use a System Browser 160
Redirect URLs 161
PKCE Extension 164
Server Support Checklist 164

16. OAuth for Browserless and Input-Constrained Devices 165
User Flow 165
Authorization Request 168
Token Request 169
Authorization Server Requirements 171
Security Considerations 173

17. Protecting Apps with PKCE 175
Authorization Request 176
Authorization Code Exchange 178

18. Token Introspection Endpoint 181
Security Considerations 185

19. Creating Documentation 187
Client Registration 187
Endpoints 188
Client Authentication 189
Sizes of Strings 189
Response Types 190
Redirect URL Restrictions 190

Default Scopes 190
Access Token Response 191
Refresh Tokens 191
Extension Grants 192

Part III. Reference

20. Terminology Reference 195
21. Differences Between OAuth 1 and 2 199
    Authentication and Signatures 200
    User Experience and Alternative Token Issuance Options 201
    Performance at Scale..203
    Bearer Tokens 203
    Short-Lived Tokens with Long-Lived Authorizations.............204
    Separation of Roles..205

22. OpenID Connect...207
    Authorization vs Authentication 207
    Building an Authentication Framework 208
    ID Tokens 209

23. IndieAuth 211
    Discovery 212
    Sign-In Flow...213
    Authorization Flow 216

24. Map of OAuth 2.0 Specs...221
    Core Specs..222
    Tokens 224
    Mobile and Other Devices 226
    Authentication and Identification 228
    Interop 229
    High Security 230
    Experimental Specs 231
    Enterprise 232

25. Tools and Libraries...233

References 237

Preface

I first got involved with OAuth in 2010 when I was building an API, and knew that I wanted third-party developers to be able to build apps on top of it. At the time, OAuth seemed incredibly intimidating. There were only a few implementations of OAuth 1 in existence, and OAuth 2.0 was still a rough draft. One night I decided to sit down with a craft beer and a paper copy of the latest draft and read it from start to finish until I understood it.

After wading through the forty-four-page spec, I learned a couple things: reading specs is not the best way to learn how OAuth works, and OAuth 2.0 wasn't nearly as complicated as I originally had thought. I began writing a simplified overview of the spec that I wished had existed when I was first learning this. I published it on my website as a blog post called "OAuth 2.0 Simplified" (*https://aaronparecki.com/oauth-2-simplified/*). This post is now viewed hundreds of thousands of times each year. It is clear that people know OAuth 2.0 is the right choice for securing their APIs, and are looking for resources to help understand it.

I had been wanting to expand this blog post into a more comprehensive guide to OAuth servers, and in 2016, I was put in touch with Okta, and we published the first version of this new guide to OAuth on *oauth.com*. In 2017, we collaborated on publishing the print edition of the book, and have published revised editions in the following years.

My hope is that this book makes OAuth 2.0 more approachable, and gives you a solid foundation of knowledge that you'll need as you continue to work with technologies on the Web.

Acknowledgments

I would especially like to thank Lindsay Brunner for her work coordinating the first two editions of this project. I would like to thank Ryan Carlson, Jamie Lee Rice, and Joël Franusic at Okta for their support. I would also like to thank the team at Okta for their work on designing the oauth.com website as well as the illustrations in this book. I would especially like to thank Karl McGuinness and Micah Silverman for their review and feedback on this content.

I also would like to thank Eran Hammer, the former editor of the OAuth 2.0 spec, William Denniss for his excellent work on the specs for native apps and browserless devices, as well as everyone else in the OAuth Working Group who has contributed to the many OAuth specs over the years.

○ ○ ○ ○ ○

Background

Before OAuth, a common pattern for granting access to your account to a third-party application was to simply give it your password and allow it to act as you. We commonly saw this with Twitter apps which would ask for your Twitter password in order to give you some stats on your account, or would ask to be able to tweet something from your account in exchange for something of value.

This pattern of applications obtaining user passwords obviously has a number of problems. Since the application would need to log in to the service as the user, these applications would often store users' passwords in plain text, making them a target for harvesting passwords. Once the application has the user's password, it has complete access to the user's account, including having access to capabilities such as changing the user's password! Another problem was that after giving an app your password, the only way you'd be able to revoke that access was by changing your password, something that users are typically reluctant to do.

Naturally, many services quickly realized the problems and limitations of this model, and sought to solve this quickly. Many services implemented things similar to OAuth 1.0. Flickr's API used what was called "FlickrAuth" which used "frobs" and "tokens". Google created "AuthSub". Facebook opted to issue each application a secret, and require the application sign each request with an md5 hash with that secret. Yahoo created "BBAuth" (Browser-Based Auth). The result was a wide variety of solutions to the problem, completely incompatible with each other, and often failing to address certain security considerations.

Around November 2006, Blaine Cook, chief architect at Twitter, was looking for a better authentication method for the Twitter API, something that didn't require users giving out their Twitter passwords to third-party apps.

> We want something like Flickr Auth / Google AuthSub / Yahoo! BBAuth, but published as an open standard, with common server and client libraries.
>
> — Blaine Cook, April 5, 2007

In 2007, a group of people working on the development of OpenID got together and created a mailing list to produce a proposal for a standard for API access control that could be used by any system, regardless of whether it used OpenID. This original group included Blaine Cook, Kellen Elliott-McCrea, Larry Halff, Tara Hunt, Ian McKeller, Chris Messina, and a few others.

In the following months, several people from Google and AOL got involved, wanting to support the effort as well. By August 2007, the first draft of the OAuth 1 spec was published, along with several implementations of API clients working against Twitter's privately-launched prototype of their OAuth API. Eran Hammer joined the project, eventually taking over as community chair and editor of the spec. By the end of the year, the community published 7 updated drafts and the OAuth Core 1.0 spec was declared final at the Internet Identity Workshop.

Over the next couple years, work on the OAuth spec moved to an IETF working group, where an effort to publish OAuth 1.1 was started. In November 2009, the editor proposed to drop work on the 1.1 revision and instead focus on a more significantly different 2.0 version.

The OAuth 2.0 spec started out as an effort to simplify and clear up many of the aspects of OAuth 1 that were difficult or confusing.

While several companies had implemented OAuth 1 APIs (namely Twitter, and later Flickr), there are some use cases, such as mobile applications, that cannot be safely implemented in OAuth 1. The goal of OAuth 2.0 was to take the knowledge learned from the first implementations of OAuth 1 and update it for the emerging mobile application use case, as well as to simplify aspects that were confusing to consumers of the APIs.

Work on the OAuth 2.0 spec began in the IETF working group, with Eran Hammer and several others named as editors of the spec. While the effort began on a strong note, it quickly became apparent that people in the group had very different goals with the spec.

The source of the contentions around the development of the OAuth 2.0 framework stemmed from the unbridgeable conflicts between the web and enterprise worlds. As work on the spec continued, most of the contributors in the web community left to go implement their products, leaving only the enterprise crowd to finish the spec.

In July 2010, the draft 10 was published, and no new drafts were published until December that year. Draft 10 still had a few people in the web community contributing, and so the spec was coming along nicely. The result was that most of the services that decided to implement an OAuth 2.0 API were reading draft 10. Most of the implementations at the time (Facebook, Salesforce, Windows Live, Google, Foursquare, etc) were all doing roughly the same thing. After launching their APIs they rarely went back and updated to newer drafts of OAuth 2.

Over the next 22 revisions of the standard, the web and enterprise contributors continued to disagree on fundamental issues. The only way to resolve the disagreements and continue making progress was to pull out the conflicting issues and put them into their own drafts, leaving holes in the spec that were called "extensible". By the final draft, so much of the core was pulled into separate documents, that the core document was renamed from being a "protocol" to being a "framework," and a disclaimer was added that "this specification is likely to produce a wide range of non-interoperable implementations."

In 2012, Eran Hammer, the primary editor of the OAuth 2.0 standard, decided he could no longer contribute to the standard and officially withdrew his name and left the working group. *http://hueniverse.com/2012/07/oauth-2-0-and-the-road-to-hell/* Naturally this stirred up a lot of attention in what was going on with the standard, which he did a good job of addressing in blog posts and at one final conference in Portland, Oregon. He ended his blog post with "I'm hoping someone will take 2.0 and produce a 10 page profile that's useful for the vast majority of web providers."

Today, if someone wants to implement OAuth 2.0 for their web service, they need to synthesize information from a number of different RFCs and drafts. The standard itself does not require a token type, and does not require any specific grant types. This means implementers must decide which they will be supporting. The standard does not even give any guidance on token string size, which ends up being one of the first questions every implementer asks when they get started. Implementers must also read the security guidance and cautions in the document and understand the implications of the decisions they are forced to make.

Interestingly, most of the web services that do implement OAuth 2.0 for their APIs come to many of the same decisions, and so most of the OAuth 2.0 APIs in existence look very similar. This book is a guide to building OAuth 2.0 APIs, with concrete recommendations based on the majority of the live implementations.

Part I
OAuth 2.0 Clients

Chapter 1
Getting Ready

In Part I of this book, we'll walk through the things you need to know when you're building an app that talks to an existing OAuth 2.0 API. Whether you're building a web app or a mobile app, there are a few things you'll need to keep in mind as we get started.

Every OAuth 2.0 service will require that you first register a new application, which also typically requires that you first sign up as a developer with the service.

Creating an Application

The registration process typically involves creating a developer account on the service's website, then entering basic information about the application such as the name, website, logo, etc. After registering the application, you'll be given a `client_id` (and a `client_secret` in some cases) that you'll use when your app interacts with the service.

One of the most important things when creating the application is to register one or more redirect URLs the application will use. The redirect URLs are where the OAuth 2.0 service will return the user to after they have authorized the application. It is critical that these are registered, otherwise it is easy to create malicious applications that can steal user data. This is covered in more detail later in this book.

Redirect URLs and State

OAuth 2.0 APIs will only redirect users to a URL that was previously registered with the service, in order to prevent redirection attacks where an authorization code or access token can be intercepted by an attacker. Some services may allow you to register multiple redirect URLs, which can help when your web app may be running on serveral different subdomains.

In order to be secure, the redirect URL must be an https endpoint to prevent the authorization code from being intercepted during the authorization process. If your redirect URL is not https, then an attacker may be able to intercept the authorization code and use it to hijack a session. The one exception to this is for apps running on the loopback interface, such as a native desktop application, or when doing local development. However even though the spec allows this exception, some OAuth services you encounter may require https redirect URLs anyway.

OAuth services should be looking for an exact match of the redirect URL. This means a redirect URL of `https://example.com/auth` would not match `https://example.com/auth?destination=account`. It is best practice to avoid using query string parameters in your redirect URL, and have it include just a path.

Some applications may have multiple places they want to start the OAuth process from, such as a login link on a home page as well as a login link when viewing some public item. For these applications, it may be tempting to try to register multiple redirect URLs, or you may think you need to be able to vary the redirect URL per request. Instead, OAuth 2.0 provides a mechanism for this, the "state" parameter.

The "state" parameter can be used to encode application state, but it must also include some amount of random data if you're not also including PKCE on page 175 parameters in the request. The state parameter is a string that is opaque to the OAuth 2.0 service, so whatever state value you pass in during the initial authorization request will be returned after the user authorizes the application. You could for example encode a redirect URL in something like a

JWT, and parse this after the user is redirected back to your application so you can take the user back to the appropriate location after they sign in.

Note that unless you are using a signed or encrypted method like JWT to encode the state parameter, you should treat it as untrusted/unvalidated data when it arrives at your redirect URL, since it's trivial for anyone to modify that parameter on the redirect back to your app.

Chapter 2

Accessing Data in an OAuth Server

In this chapter, we'll walk through how to access your data at an existing OAuth 2.0 server. For this example, we'll use the GitHub API, and build a simple application that will list all repositories the logged-in user has created.

Create an Application

Before we can begin, we'll need to create an application on GitHub in order to get a client ID and client secret.

On GitHub.com, from the "Settings" page, click on the "Developer Settings" link in the sidebar. You will end up on *https://github.com/settings/developers*. From there, click "New OAuth App" and you will be presented with a short form, as shown in Figure 2-1.

Fill out the required information, including the callback URL. If you are developing an application locally, you'll have to use a local address for the callback URL. Since GitHub allows only one registered callback URL per application, it is useful to create two applications, one for development, and a separate one for production.

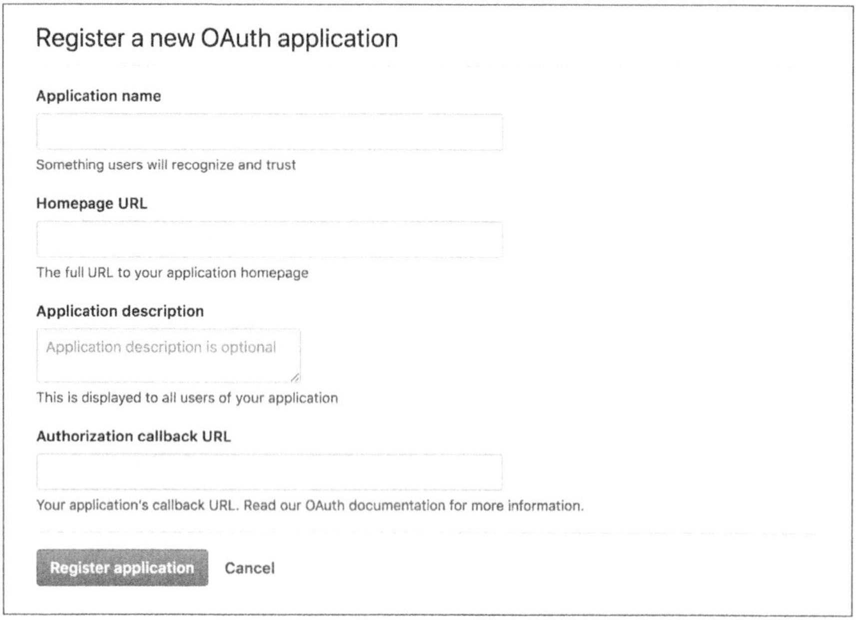

Figure 2-1: Register a new OAuth application on GitHub

After completing this form, you'll be taken to a page where you can see the client ID and secret issued to your application, shown in Figure 2-2.

The client ID is considered public information, and is used to build authorization URLs, or can be included in the JavaScript source code of a web page. The client secret **must** be kept confidential. Don't commit this to your git repository or include it in any JavaScript files!

OAuth 2 Example App

aaronpk owns this application.   **Transfer ownership**

You can list your application in the GitHub Marketplace so that other users can discover it.   **List this application in the Marketplace**

0 users

Client ID
0d74d0134cb9a1102e5d

Client Secret
[redacted]

Revoke all user tokens   **Reset client secret**

Application logo

Upload new logo
You can also drag and drop a picture from your computer.

Badge background color

#ffffff

The hex value of the badge background color.

Application name

OAuth 2 Example App

Something users will recognize and trust

Homepage URL

https://example-app.com

The full URL to your application homepage

Application description

This is a sample app for testing the GitHub API

This is displayed to all users of your application

Authorization callback URL

https://example-app.com/callback

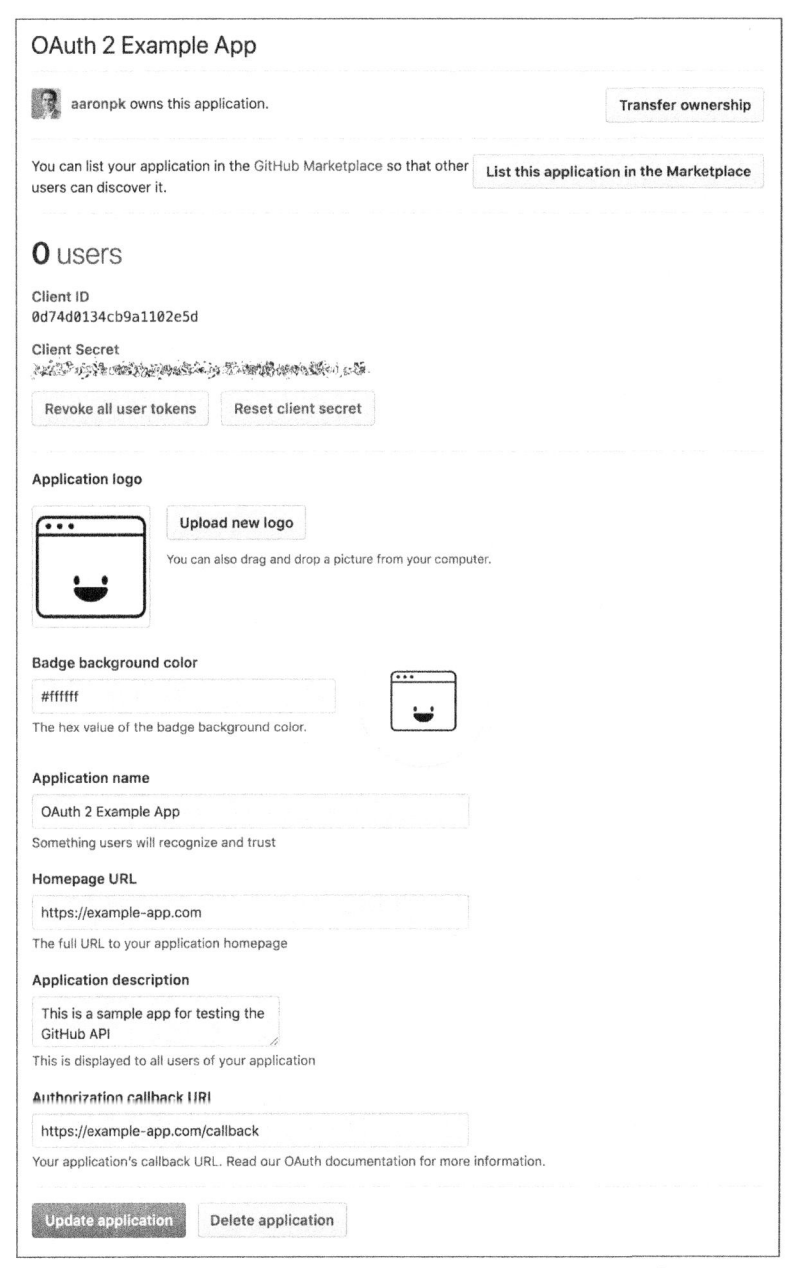

Your application's callback URL. Read our OAuth documentation for more information.

Update application   **Delete application**

Figure 2-2: GitHub application has been created

Setting Up the Environment

This example code is written in PHP with no external packages required and no framework needed. Hopefully this makes it easy to translate to other languages if desired. To follow along with this example code, you can place it all in a single PHP file.

Create a new folder and create an empty file in that folder called `index.php`. From the command line, run `php -S localhost:8000` from inside that folder, and you'll be able to visit *http://localhost:8000* in your browser to run your code. All the code in the examples below should be added to this `index.php` file.

To make things easier for us, let's define a method, `apiRequest()` which is a simple wrapper around cURL. This function will include the `Accept` and `User-Agent` headers that GitHub's API requires, and automatically decode the JSON response. If we have an access token in the session, it will send the proper OAuth header with the access token as well, in order to make authenticated requests.

```php
function apiRequest($url, $post=FALSE, $headers=array()) {
  $ch = curl_init($url);
  curl_setopt($ch, CURLOPT_RETURNTRANSFER, TRUE);

  if($post)
    curl_setopt($ch, CURLOPT_POSTFIELDS, http_build_query($post));

  $headers = [
    'Accept: application/vnd.github.v3+json, application/json',
    'User-Agent: https://example-app.com/'
  ];

  if(isset($_SESSION['access_token']))
    $headers[] = 'Authorization: Bearer '.$_SESSION['access_token'];

  curl_setopt($ch, CURLOPT_HTTPHEADER, $headers);

  $response = curl_exec($ch);
  return json_decode($response, true);
}
```

Now let's set up a few variables we'll need for the OAuth process.

```
// Fill these out with the values from GitHub
$githubClientID = '';
$githubClientSecret = '';

// This is the URL we'll send the user to first
// to get their authorization
$authorizeURL = 'https://github.com/login/oauth/authorize';

// This is the endpoint we'll request an access token from
$tokenURL = 'https://github.com/login/oauth/access_token';

// This is the GitHub base URL for API requests
$apiURLBase = 'https://api.github.com/';

// The URL for this script, used as the redirect URL
$baseURL = 'https://' . $_SERVER['SERVER_NAME']
    . $_SERVER['PHP_SELF'];

// Start a session so we have a place to
// store things between redirects
session_start();
```

First, let's set up the "logged-in" and "logged-out" views. This will show a simple message indicating whether the user is logged in or logged out.

```
// If there is an access token in the session
// the user is already logged in
if(!isset($_GET['action'])) {
  if(!empty($_SESSION['access_token'])) {
    echo '<h3>Logged In</h3>';
    echo '<p><a href="?action=repos">View Repos</a></p>';
    echo '<p><a href="?action=logout">Log Out</a></p>';
  } else {
    echo '<h3>Not logged in</h3>';
    echo '<p><a href="?action=login">Log In</a></p>';
  }
  die();
}
```

The logged-out view contains a link to our login URL which starts the OAuth process.

Authorization Request

Now that we have the necessary variables set up, let's start the OAuth process.

The first thing we'll have people do is visit this page with `?action=login` in the query string to kick off the process.

Note the scopes we are asking for in this request include `user` and `public_repo`. This means the app will be able to read the user profile information as well as have access to public repos.

```php
// Start the login process by sending the user
// to GitHub's authorization page
if(isset($_GET['action']) && $_GET['action'] == 'login') {
  unset($_SESSION['access_token']);

  // Generate a random hash and store in the session
  $_SESSION['state'] = bin2hex(random_bytes(16));

  $params = array(
    'response_type' => 'code',
    'client_id' => $githubClientID,
    'redirect_uri' => $baseURL,
    'scope' => 'user public_repo',
    'state' => $_SESSION['state']
  );

  // Redirect the user to GitHub's authorization page
  header('Location: '.$authorizeURL.'?'.http_build_query($params));
  die();
}
```

It's important to generate a "state" parameter to use to protect the client from CSRF attacks. This is a random string that the client generates and stores in the session. GitHub will redirect the user back here with the state in the query string, so we can verify it matches the state stored in the session before exchanging the authorization code for an access token.

We build up the authorization URL and then send the user there. The URL contains our public client ID, the redirect URL which we previously registered with GitHub, the scope we're requesting, and the state parameter.

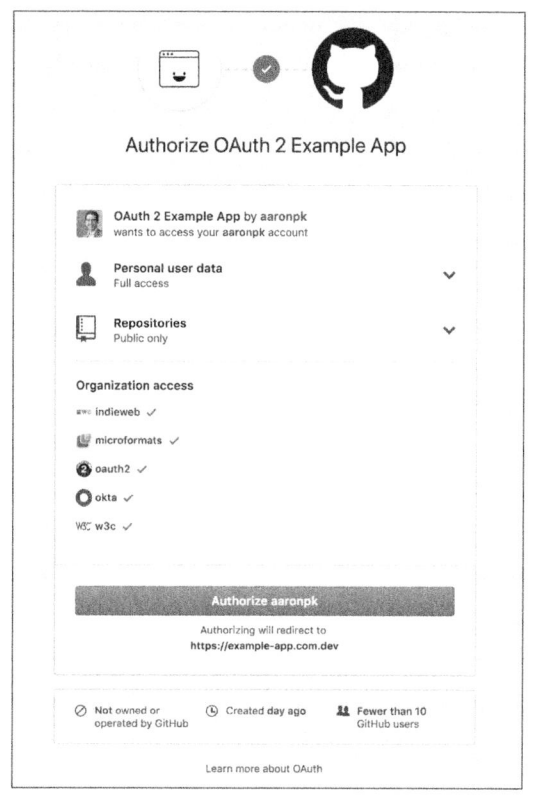

Figure 2-3: GitHub's Authorization Request

At this point, the user will see GitHub's OAuth authorization prompt, illustrated in Figure 2-3.

When the user approves the request, they will be redirected back to our page with code and state parameters in the request. The next step is to exchange the authorization code for an access token.

Obtaining an Access Token

When the user is redirected back to our app, there will be a code and state parameter in the query string. The state parameter will be the same as the one we set in the initial authorization request, and is meant for our app to check that it matches before continuing. This helps our app avoid being tricked into sending an attacker's authorization code to GitHub, as well as prevents CSRF attacks.

```
// When GitHub redirects the user back here,
// there will be a "code" and "state" parameter in the query string
if(isset($_GET['code'])) {
  // Verify the state matches our stored state
  if(!isset($_GET['state'])
    || $_SESSION['state'] != $_GET['state']) {

    header('Location: ' . $baseURL . '?error=invalid_state');
    die();
  }

  // Exchange the auth code for an access token
  $token = apiRequest($tokenURL, array(
    'grant_type' => 'authorization_code',
    'client_id' => $githubClientID,
    'client_secret' => $githubClientSecret,
    'redirect_uri' => $baseURL,
    'code' => $_GET['code']
  ));
  $_SESSION['access_token'] = $token['access_token'];

  header('Location: ' . $baseURL);
  die();
}
```

Here we are sending a request to GitHub's token endpoint to exchange the authorization code for an access token. The request contains our public client ID as well as the private client secret. We also send the same redirect URL as before along with the authorization code.

If everything checks out, GitHub generates an access token and returns it in the response. We store the access token in the session and redirect to the home page, and the user is logged in.

The response from GitHub will look like the below.

```
{
  "access_token": "e2f8c8e136c73b1e909bb1021b3b4c29",
  "token_type": "Bearer",
  "scope": "public_repo,user"
}
```

Our code has extracted the access token and saved it in the session. The next time you visit the page, it recognizes that there's already an access token and shows the logged-in view we created earlier.

Note: We have not included any error handling code in this example for simplicity's sake. In reality, you'd check for errors returned from GitHub and display an appropriate message to the user.

Making API Requests

Now that our app has a GitHub access token for the user, we can use it to make API requests. Let's add a new section to our application that will run when the user clicks the "View Repos" link we created earlier.

Remember the `apiRequest` function we set up earlier? That's where the access token is included in the HTTP request. The request this code will make will include the access token in the HTTP `Authorization` header, as illustrated in the example below.

```
GET /user/repos?sort=created&direction=desc HTTP/1.1
Host: api.github.com
Accept: application/vnd.github.v3+json
User-Agent: https://example-app.com/
Authorization: Bearer e2f8c8e136c73b1e909bb1021b3b4c29
```

The code below will take the access token and use it in a request to list the user's repositories. It will then output a list of repositories and link to each one.

```
if(isset($_GET['action']) && $_GET['action'] == 'repos') {
  // Find all repos created by the authenticated user
  $repos = apiRequest($apiURLBase.'user/repos?'.http_build_query([
    'sort' => 'created', 'direction' => 'desc'
  ]));

  echo '<ul>';
  foreach($repos as $repo)
    echo '<li><a href="' . $repo['html_url'] . '">'
      . $repo['name'] . '</a></li>';
  echo '</ul>';
}
```

Chapter 2: Accessing Data in an OAuth Server

That's it! You can now use the access token to make API requests to any of the API endpoints on GitHub! You can see the full documentation of GitHub's API at *https://developer.github.com/v3/*.

Download the Sample Code

You can download the complete sample code used in this example from GitHub at *https://github.com/aaronpk/sample-oauth2-client*.

Chapter 3
Signing In with Google

Despite OAuth being an *authorization* protocol rather than an *authentication* protocol, it is often used as the basis for authentication workflows anyway. A typical use of many common OAuth APIs is just to identify the user at the computer when logging in to a third-party app.

Authentication and authorization are often confused with each other, but can be more easily understood if you think about them from the perspective of an application. An app that is authenticating users is just verifying who the user is. An app that is authorizing users is trying to gain access or modify something that belongs to the user.

OAuth was designed as an authorization protocol, so the end result of every OAuth flow is the app obtains an access token in order to be able to access or modify something about the user's account. The access token itself says nothing about *who* the user is.

There are several ways different services provide a way for an app to find out the identity of the user. A simple way is for the API to provide a "user info" endpoint which will return the authenticated user's name and other profile info when an API call is made with an access token. While this is not something that is part of the OAuth standard, it's a common approach many services have taken. A more advanced and standardized approach is to use OpenID Connect, an OAuth 2.0 extension. OpenID Connect is covered in more detail in Chapter 22.

This chapter will walk through using a simplified OpenID Connect workflow with the Google API to identify the user who signed in to your application.

Create an Application

Before we can begin, we'll need to create an application in the Google API Console in order to get a client ID and client secret, and register the redirect URL.

Visit *https://console.developers.google.com/* and create a new project. You'll also need to create OAuth 2.0 credentials for the project since Google does not do that automatically. From the sidebar, click the **Credentials** tab, then click **Create credentials** and choose **OAuth client ID** from the dropdown.

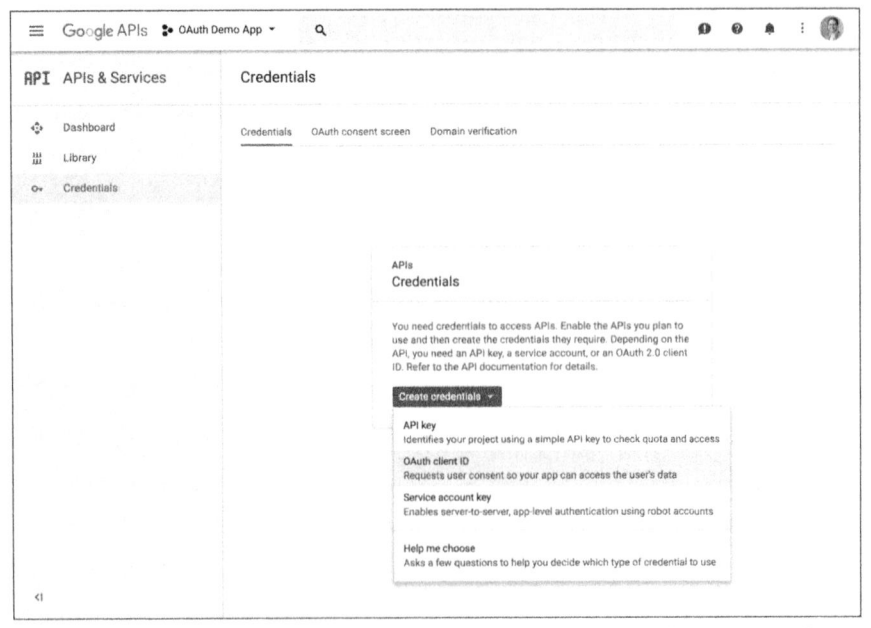

Figure 3-1: Create Credentials for your App on the Google API Console

The Google Console will prompt for some information about your application such as the product name, a home page, and a logo. On the next page, select **Web application** type, and enter the redirect URL where the script we'll build next will live. You will then receive a client ID and secret.

Setting Up the Environment

This example code is written in PHP with no external packages required and no framework needed. Hopefully this makes it easy to translate to other languages if desired. To follow along with this example code, you can place it all in a single PHP file.

Create a new folder and create an empty file in that folder called `index.php`. From the command line, run `php -S localhost:8000` from inside that folder, and you'll be able to visit *http://localhost:8000* in your browser to run your code. All the code in the examples below should be added to this `index.php` file.

Let's set up a few variables we'll need for the OAuth process, adding the client ID and secret we got from Google when we created the application.

```php
// Fill these out with the values you got from Google
$googleClientID = '';
$googleClientSecret = '';

// This is the URL we'll send the user to first
// to get their authorization
$authorizeURL = 'https://accounts.google.com/o/oauth2/v2/auth';

// This is Google's OpenID Connect token endpoint
$tokenURL = 'https://www.googleapis.com/oauth2/v4/token';

// The URL for this script, used as the redirect URL
$baseURL = 'https://' . $_SERVER['SERVER_NAME']
    . $_SERVER['PHP_SELF'];

// Start a session so we have a place
// to store things between redirects
session_start();
```

With those variables defined, and the session started, let's set up the logged in and logged out pages. We'll show a super simple page that just indicates whether the user is logged in or not, and has a link to log in or log out.

```
// If there is a user ID in the session
// the user is already logged in
if(!isset($_GET['action'])) {
  if(!empty($_SESSION['user_id'])) {
    echo '<h3>Logged In</h3>';
    echo '<p>User ID: '.$_SESSION['user_id'].'</p>';
    echo '<p>Email: '.$_SESSION['email'].'</p>';
    echo '<p><a href="?action=logout">Log Out</a></p>';

    // Fetch user info from Google's userinfo endpoint
    echo '<h3>User Info</h3>';
    echo '<pre>';
    $ch = curl_init('https://www.googleapis.com/oauth2/v3/userinfo');
    curl_setopt($ch, CURLOPT_HTTPHEADER, [
      'Authorization: Bearer '.$_SESSION['access_token']
    ]);
    curl_exec($ch);
    echo '</pre>';

  } else {
    echo '<h3>Not logged in</h3>';
    echo '<p><a href="?action=login">Log In</a></p>';
  }
  die();
}
```

The logged-out view contains a link to our login URL which starts the flow.

Authorization Request

Now that we have the necessary variables set up, let's start the OAuth process.

The first thing we'll have people do is visit this page with ?action=login in the query string to kick off the process.

Note that scopes in this request are now OpenID Connect scopes, "openid email", indicating that we are not requesting access to the user's Google data, just wanting to know who they are.

Also note that we are using the `response_type=code` parameter to indicate that we want Google to return an authorization code that we'll exchange for the id_token later.

```php
// Start the login process by sending the user
// to Google's authorization page
if(isset($_GET['action']) && $_GET['action'] == 'login') {
  unset($_SESSION['user_id']);

  // Generate a random string and store in the session
  $_SESSION['state'] = bin2hex(random_bytes(16));

  $params = array(
    'response_type' => 'code',
    'client_id' => $googleClientID,
    'redirect_uri' => $baseURL,
    'scope' => 'openid email',
    'state' => $_SESSION['state']
  );

  // Redirect the user to Google's authorization page
  header('Location: '.$authorizeURL.'?'.http_build_query($params));
  die();
}
```

It's important to generate a "state" parameter to use to protect the client from CSRF attacks. This is a random string that the client generates and stores in the session. Our app will verify that that state parameter in the redirect from Google matches the one that was created at the start of the flow.

We build up an authorization URL and then send the user there. The URL contains our public client ID, the redirect URL which we previously registered with Google, the scope we're requesting, and the "state" parameter.

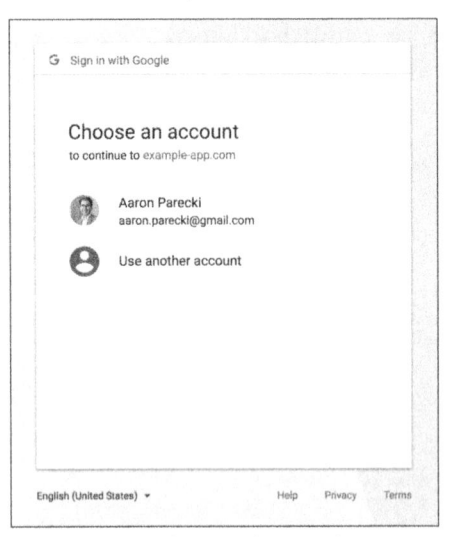

Figure 3-2: Google's Authorization Request

If the user is already logged in to Google, they'll see an account chooser screen as shown in Figure 3-2 asking them to choose an existing account or use a different account. Notice that this screen does not look like a typical OAuth screen, because the user isn't granting any permissions to the application, it's just trying to identify them.

When the user selects an account, they will be redirected back to our page with `code` and `state` parameters in the request. The next step is to exchange the authorization code for an access token at the Google API.

Getting an ID Token

When the user is redirected back to our app, there will be a `code` and `state` parameter in the query string. The `state` parameter will be the same as the one we set in the initial authorization request, and is meant for our app to check that it matches before continuing. This helps protect our app from CSRF attacks.

```php
// When Google redirects the user back here, there will
// be a "code" and "state" parameter in the query string
if(isset($_GET['code'])) {
  // Verify the state matches our stored state
  if(!isset($_GET['state']) || $_SESSION['state'] != $_GET['state']) {
    header('Location: ' . $baseURL . '?error=invalid_state');
    die();
  }

  // Exchange the authorization code for an access token
  $ch = curl_init($tokenURL);
  curl_setopt($ch, CURLOPT_RETURNTRANSFER, true);
  curl_setopt($ch, CURLOPT_POSTFIELDS, http_build_query([
    'grant_type' => 'authorization_code',
    'client_id' => $googleClientID,
    'client_secret' => $googleClientSecret,
    'redirect_uri' => $baseURL,
    'code' => $_GET['code']
  ]));
  $response = json_decode(curl_exec($ch), true);

  // ... fill in from the code in the next section
}
```

This code first checks that the "state" returned from Google matches the state we stored in our session.

We build up a POST request to Google's token endpoint containing our app's client ID and secret, as well as the authorization code that Google sent back to us in the query string.

Google will verify our request, and then respond with both an access token as well as an ID token. The response will look like the below.

```
{
  "access_token": "ya29.Glins-oLtuljNVfthQU2bpJVJPTu",
  "token_type": "Bearer",
  "expires_in": 3600,
  "id_token": "eyJhbGciOiJSUzI1NiIsImtpZCI6ImFmZmM2MjkwN
?FANDYxODJhZGMxZmE0ZTgxZmRiYTYzMTBkY2U2M2YifQ.eyJhenAi
OiIyNzIxOTYwNjkxNzMtZm81ZWI0MXQzbmR1cTZ1ZXRkc2pkdWdzZX
V0ZnBtc3QuYXBwcy5nb29nbGV1c2VyY29udGVudC5jb20iLCJhdWQi
OiIyNzIxOTYwNjkxNzMtZm81ZWI0MXQzbmR1cTZ1ZXRkc2pkdWdzZX
V0ZnBtc3QuYXBwcy5nb29nbGV1c2VyY29udGVudC5jb20iLCJzdWIi
OiIxMTc4NDc5MTI4NzU5MTM5MDU0OTMiLCJlbWFpbCI6ImFhcm9uLn
BhcmVja2lAZ21haWwuY29tIiwiZW1haWxfdmVyaWZpZWQiOnRydWUs
```

```
    ImF0X2hhc2giOiJpRVljNDBUR0luUkhoVEJidWRncEpRIiwiZXhwIj
    oxNTI0NTk5MDU2LCJpc3MiOiJodHRwczovL2FjY291bnRzLmdvb2ds
    ZS5jb20iLCJpYXQiOjE1MjQ1OTU0NTZ9.ho2czp_1JWsglJ9jN8gCg
    WfxDi2gY4X5-QcT56RUGkgh5BJaaWdlrRhhN_eNuJyN3HRPhvVA_KJ
    Vy1tMltTVd2OQ6VkxgBNfBsThG_zLPZriw7a1lANblarwxLZID4fXD
    YG-O8U-gw4xb-NIsOzx6xsxRBdfKKniavuEg56Sd3eKYyqrMA0DWnI
    agqLiKE6kpZkaGImIpLcIxJPF0-yeJTMt_p1NoJF7uguHHLYr6752h
    qppnBpMjFL2YMDVeg3jl1y5DeSKNPh6cZ8H2p4Xb2UIrJguGbQHVIJ
    vtm_AspRjrmaTUQKrzXDRCfDROSUU-h7XKIWRrEd2-W9UkV5oCg"
}
```

The access token should be treated as an opaque string. It has no significant meaning to your app other than being able to use it to make API requests.

The ID token has a specific structure that your app can parse to find out the user data of who signed in. The ID token is a JWT, explained in more detail in Chapter 22, *OpenID Connect,* (page 209). You can paste the JWT from Google into a site like *example-app.com/base64* to quickly show you the contents, or you can base64 decode the middle part between the two .'s to see the user data which we'll do next.

Verifying the User Info

Normally, it's critical that you validate an ID token before trusting any of the information inside it. This is because in other OpenID Connect flows your app will get an ID token over an untrusted channel such as a browser redirect.

In this case, you got the ID token from an HTTPS connection to Google using the client secret to authenticate the request, so you can be confident that the ID token you obtained did in fact come from Google and not an attacker. With this in mind, and I know it seems unsafe at first, it's okay to decode the ID token without validating it. Even Google says so. *https://developers.google.com/identity/ protocols/OpenIDConnect#obtainuserinfo.*

Take a look at the JWT above. It's made up of three parts, each separated by a period. We can split the string on the dots, and then take the middle piece. The middle piece is a base64-encoded JSON string containing the data about the user. Below is an example of the data in the JWT.

```
{
  "azp": "272196069173.apps.googleusercontent.com",
  "aud": "272196069173.apps.googleusercontent.com",
  "sub": "110248495921238986420",
  "hd": "okta.com",
  "email": "aaron.parecki@okta.com",
  "email_verified": true,
  "at_hash": "0bzSP5g7IfV3HXoLwYS3Lg",
  "exp": 1524601669,
  "iss": "https://accounts.google.com",
  "iat": 1524598069
}
```

All we really care about for this demo are the two properties `sub` and `email`. The `sub` (subject) property contains the unique user identifier of the user who signed in. We'll extract that and store it in the session, which will indicate to our app that the user is signed in.

We'll also store the ID token and access token in the session so we can use them later, to show an alternative way of getting the user info.

```
// ... continuing from the previous code sample, insert this

// Split the JWT string into three parts
$jwt = explode('.', $data['id_token']);

// Extract the middle part, base64 decode, then json_decode it
$userinfo = json_decode(base64_decode($jwt[1]), true);

$_SESSION['user_id'] = $userinfo['sub'];
$_SESSION['email'] = $userinfo['email'];

// While we're at it, let's store the access token and id token
// so we can use them later
$_SESSION['access_token'] = $data['access_token'];
$_SESSION['id_token'] = $data['id_token'];

header('Location: ' . $baseURL);
die();
}
```

Now you'll be redirected back to the app's home page, where we'll show you the user ID and email using the code we created at the beginning.

```php
echo '<p>User ID: '.$_SESSION['user_id'].'</p>';
echo '<p>Email: '.$_SESSION['email'].'</p>';
```

Using the ID Token to Retrieve User Info

Google provides an additional API endpoint, called the tokeninfo endpoint, which you can use to look up the ID token details instead of parsing it yourself. This is not recommended for production applications, as it requires an additional HTTP round trip, but can be useful for testing and troubleshooting.

Google's tokeninfo endpoint is at `https://www.googleapis.com/oauth2/v3/tokeninfo`, as found in their OpenID Connect discovery document at `https://accounts.google.com/.well-known/openid-configuration`. To look up the info for the ID token we received, make a GET request to the tokeninfo endpoint with the ID token in the query string.

```
https://www.googleapis.com/oauth2/v3/tokeninfo?id_token=eyJ...
```

The response will be a JSON object with a similar list of properties that were included in the JWT itself.

```json
{
  "azp": "272196069173.apps.googleusercontent.com",
  "aud": "272196069173.apps.googleusercontent.com",
  "sub": "110248495921238986420",
  "hd": "okta.com",
  "email": "aaron.parecki@okta.com",
  "email_verified": "true",
  "at_hash": "NUuq_yggZYi_2-13hJSOXw",
  "exp": "1524681857",
  "iss": "https://accounts.google.com",
  "iat": "1524678257",
  "alg": "RS256",
  "kid": "affc62907a446182adc1fa4e81fdba6310dce63f"
}
```

Using the Access Token to Retrieve User Info

As mentioned before, many OAuth 2.0 services also provide an endpoint to retrieve the user info of the user who logged in. This is part of the OpenID Connect standard, and the endpoint will be part of the service's OpenID Connect Discovery Document.

Google's userinfo endpoint is https://www.googleapis.com/oauth2/v3/userinfo. In this case, you use the access token rather than the ID token to look up the user info. Make a GET request to that endpoint and pass the access token in the HTTP Authorization header like you normally would when making an OAuth 2.0 API request.

```
GET /oauth2/v3/userinfo
Host: www.googleapis.com
Authorization: Bearer ya29.Gl-oBRPLiI9IrSRA70...
```

The response will be a JSON object with several properties about the user. The response will always include the sub key, which is the unique identifier for the user. Google also returns the user's profile information such as name (first and last), profile photo URL, gender, locale, profile URL, and email. The server can also add its own claims, such as Google's hd showing the "hosted domain" of the account when using a G Suite account.

```
{
  "sub": "110248495921238986420",
  "name": "Aaron Parecki",
  "given_name": "Aaron",
  "family_name": "Parecki",
  "picture": "https://lh4.googleusercontent.com/-kw-iMgD
    _j34/AAAAAAAAAAI/AAAAAAAAAc/P1YY91tzesU/photo.jpg",
  "email": "aaron.parecki@okta.com",
  "email_verified": true,
  "locale": "en",
  "hd": "okta.com"
}
```

Download the Sample Code

You can download the complete sample code used in this example from GitHub at *https://github.com/aaronpk/sample-oauth2-client*.

You've seen three different ways to get the user's profile info after the user signs in. So which one should you use and when?

For performance-sensitive applications where you might be reading ID tokens on every request or using them to maintain a session, you should definitely validate the ID token locally rather than making a network request. Google's API docs *(https://developers.google.com/identity/protocols/OpenIDConnect#validatinganidtoken)* provide a good guide on the details of validating ID tokens offline.

If all you're doing is trying to find the user's name and email after they sign in, then extracting the data from the ID token and storing it in your application session is the easiest and most straightforward option.

Chapter 4
Server-Side Apps

Server-side apps are the most common type of application encountered when dealing with OAuth servers. These apps run on a web server where the source code of the application is not available to the public, so they can maintain the confidentiality of their client secret.

Figure 4-1 illustrates a typical example where the user interacts with their browser which is communicating with the client. The client and the API server have a separate secure communications channel between them. The user's browser never makes a request directly to the API server, everything goes through the client first.

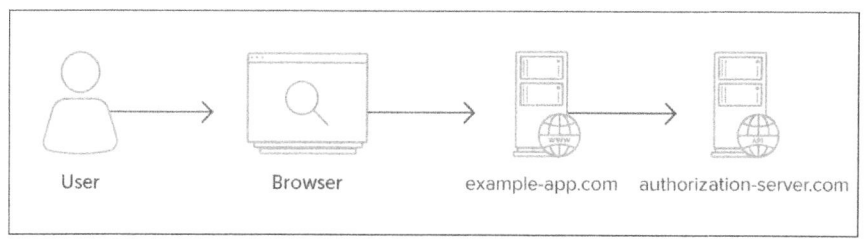

Figure 4-1: The app's server communicates with the API

Server-side apps use the `authorization_code` grant type. In this flow, after the user authorizes the application, the application receives an "authorization code" which it can then exchange for an access token.

Authorization Code Flow

The authorization code is a temporary code that the client will exchange for an access token. The code itself is obtained from the authorization server where the user gets a chance to see what the information the client is requesting, and approve or deny the request.

The authorization code flow offers a few benefits over the other grant types. When the user authorizes the application, they are redirected back to the application with a temporary code in the URL. The application exchanges that code for the access token. When the application makes the request for the access token, that request can be authenticated with the client secret, which reduces the risk of an attacker intercepting the authorization code and using it themselves. This also means the access token is never visible to the user or their browser, so it is the most secure way to pass the token back to the application, reducing the risk of the token leaking to someone else.

The first step of the web flow is to request authorization from the user. This is accomplished by creating an authorization request link for the user to click on.

The authorization URL is usually in a format such as:

```
https://authorization-server.com/oauth/authorize
?client_id=a17c21ed
&response_type=code
&state=5ca75bd30
&redirect_uri=https%3A%2F%2Fexample-app.com%2Fauth
&scope=photos
```

The exact URL endpoint will be specified by the service to which you are connecting, but the parameter names will always be the same.

Note that you will most likely first need to register your redirect URL at the service before it will be accepted. This also means you can't change your redirect URL per request. Instead, you can use the `state` parameter to customize the request. See below for more information.

After the user visits the authorization page, the service shows the user an explanation of the request, including application name, scope, etc. (See "approves the request" on page 47 for an example screenshot.) If the user clicks "approve", the server will redirect back to the app, with a "code" and the same "state" parameter you provided in the query string parameter. It is important to note that this is not an access token. The only thing you can do with the authorization code is to make a request to get an access token.

> **OAuth Security**
>
> *Up until 2019, the OAuth 2.0 spec only recommended using the PKCE extension for mobile and JavaScript apps. The latest OAuth Security BCP now recommends using PKCE also for server-side apps, as it provides some additional benefits there as well. It is likely to take some time before common OAuth services adapt to this new recommendation, but if you're building a server from scratch you should definitely support PKCE for all types of clients.*

Authorization Request Parameters

The following parameters are used to make the authorization request. You should build a query string with the below parameters, appending that to the application's authorization endpoint obtained from its documentation.

`response_type=code`

`response_type` is set to `code` indicating that you want an authorization code as the response.

`client_id`

The `client_id` is the identifier for your app. You will have received a client_id when first registering your app with the service.

Chapter 4: Server-Side Apps

`redirect_uri` (optional)

The `redirect_uri` may be optional depending on the API, but is highly recommended. This is the URL to which you want the user to be redirected after the authorization is complete. This must match the redirect URL that you have previously registered with the service.

`scope` (optional)

Include one or more scope values (space-separated) to request additional levels of access. The values will depend on the particular service.

`state`

The `state` parameter serves two functions. When the user is redirected back to your app, whatever value you include as the state will also be included in the redirect. This gives your app a chance to persist data between the user being directed to the authorization server and back again, such as using the state parameter as a session key. This may be used to indicate what action in the app to perform after authorization is complete, for example, indicating which of your app's pages to redirect to after authorization.

The state parameter also serves as a CSRF protection mechanism if it contains a random value per request. When the user is redirected back to your app, double check that the state value matches what you set it to originally.

PKCE

If the service supports PKCE for web server apps, include the PKCE challenge and challenge method here as well. This is described in a complete example in Single-Page Apps on page 53 and Mobile Apps on page 65.

Combine all of these query string parameters into the authorization URL, and direct the user's browser there. Typically apps will put these parameters into a login button, or will send this URL as an HTTP redirect from the app's own login URL.

The user approves the request

After the user is taken to the service and sees the request, they will either allow or deny the request. If they allow the request, they will be redirected back to the redirect URL specified along with an authorization code in the query string. The app then needs to exchange this authorization code for an access token.

Exchange the authorization code for an access token

To exchange the authorization code for an access token, the app makes a POST request to the service's token endpoint. The request will have the following parameters.

grant_type (required)

The `grant_type` parameter must be set to "authorization_code".

code (required)

This parameter is for the authorization code received from the authorization server which will be in the query string parameter "code" in this request.

redirect_uri (possibly required)

If the redirect URL was included in the initial authorization request, it must be included in the token request as well, and must be identical. Some services support registering multiple redirect URLs, and some require the redirect URL to be specified on each request. Check the service's documentation for the specifics.

Client Authentication (required)

The service will require the client authenticate itself when making the request for an access token. Typically services support client authentication via HTTP Basic Auth with the client's `client_id` and `client_secret`. However, some services support authentication by accepting the `client_id` and `client_secret` as POST body parameters. Check the service's documentation to find out what the service expects, since the OAuth 2.0 spec leaves this decision up to the service.

More advanced OAuth servers may also require other forms of client authentication such as mTLS or `private_key_jwt`. Refer to the service's own documentation for those examples.

PKCE Code Verifier

If the service supports PKCE for web server apps, then the client will need to include the followup PKCE parameter when exchanging the authorization code as well. Again, see Single-Page Apps on page 53 and Mobile Apps on page 65 for a complete example of using the PKCE extension.

Example Flow

The following step-by-step example illustrates using the authorization code flow with PKCE.

Step-by-step

The high level overview is this:

- Create a log-in link with the app's client ID, redirect URL, state, and PKCE code challenge parameters
- The user sees the authorization prompt and approves the request
- The user is redirected back to the app's server with an auth code

- The app exchanges the auth code for an access token

The app initiates the authorization request

The app initiates the flow by crafting a URL containing client ID, scope, state and PKCE code verifier. The app can put this into an <a href=""> tag.

```
<a href="https://authorization-server.com/oauth/authorize
?response_type=code
&client_id=mRkZGFjM
&state=5ca75bd30
&scope=photos
&code_challenge=hKpKupTM391pE10xfQiorMxXarRKAHRhTfH_xkGf7U4
&code_challenge_method=S256
">Connect Your Account</a>
```

Note that this is not an HTTP call your application is making, instead this is a URL that the user will click on to redirect their browser to the OAuth server.

The user approves the request

Upon being directed to the authorization server, the user sees the authorization request shown in Figure 4-2. If the user approves the request, they will be redirected back to the app along with the auth code and state parameters.

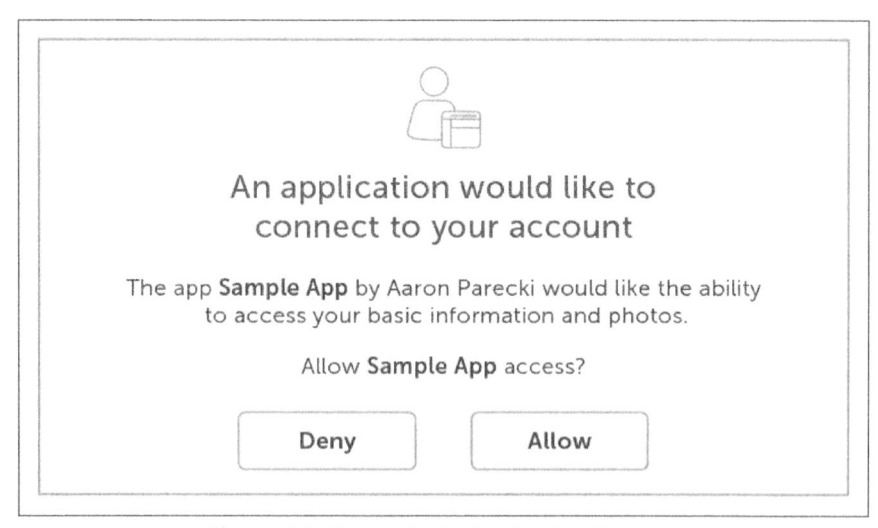

Figure 4-2: Example Authorization Request

The service redirects the user back to the app

The service sends a redirect header redirecting the user's browser back to the app that made the request. The redirect will include a "code" in the URL and the original "state".

```
https://example-app.com/cb?code=Yzk5ZDczMzR&state=5ca75bd30
```

(This will actually be sent back as an HTTP response from the authorization server to the user's browser, *not* to your application. The actual HTTP response isn't shown here because it is not significant to the code you write in your application.)

The app exchanges the auth code for an access token

Finally the application uses the authorization code to get an access token by making an HTTPS POST request to the authorization server's token endpoint.

```
POST /oauth/token HTTP/1.1
Host: authorization-server.com

grant_type=authorization_code
&code=Yzk5ZDczMzR
&redirect_uri=https://example-app.com/cb
&client_id=mRkZGFjM
&client_secret=ZGVmMjMz
&code_verifier=Th7UHJdLswIYQxwSg29DbK1a_d9o41uNMTRmuH0PM8zyoMAQ
```

The authorization server validates the request and responds with an access token and optional refresh token if the access token will expire.

Response:

```
{
  "access_token": "AYjcyMzY3ZDhiNmJkNTY",
  "refresh_token": "RjY2NjM5NzA2OWJjuE7c",
  "token_type": "Bearer",
  "expires_in": 3600
}
```

Possible Errors

There are several cases where you may get an error response during authorization.

Errors are indicated by redirecting back to the provided redirect URL with additional parameters in the query string. There will always be an error parameter, and the redirect may also include `error_description` and `error_uri`.

For example,

```
https://example-app.com/cb?error=invalid_scope
```

Despite the fact that servers return an `error_description` key, the error description is not intended to be displayed to the user. Instead, you should present the user with your own error message. This allows you to tell the user an appropriate action to take to correct the problem, and also gives you a chance to localize the error messages if you're building a multi-language website.

Invalid redirect URL

If the redirect URL provided is invalid, the authorization server will not redirect to it. Instead, it may display a message to the user describing the problem instead.

Unrecognized `client_id`

If the client ID is not recognized, the authorization server will not redirect the user. Instead, it may display a message describing the problem.

The user denies the request

If the user denies the authorization request, the server will redirect the user back to the redirect URL with `error=access_denied` in the query string, and no code will be present. It is up to the app to decide what to display to the user at this point.

Invalid parameters

If one or more parameters are invalid, such as a required value is missing, or the `response_type` parameter is wrong, the server will redirect to the redirect URL and include query string parameters describing the problem. The other possible values for the error parameter are:

`invalid_request`: The request is missing a required parameter, includes an invalid parameter value, or is otherwise malformed.

`unauthorized_client`: The client is not authorized to request an authorization code using this method.

`unsupported_response_type`: The authorization server does not support obtaining an authorization code using this method.

`invalid_scope`: The requested scope is invalid, unknown, or malformed.

`server_error`: The authorization server encountered an unexpected condition which prevented it from fulfilling the request.

`temporarily_unavailable`: The authorization server is currently unable to handle the request due to a temporary overloading or maintenance of the server.

In addition, the server may include parameters `error_description` and `error_uri` with additional information about the error.

User Experience and Security Considerations

In order for the authorization code grant to be secure, the authorization page must appear in a web browser the user is familiar with, and must not be embedded in an iframe popup or an embedded browser in a mobile app. If it could be embedded in another website, the user would have no way of verifying it is the legitimate service and is not a phishing attempt.

If an app wants to use the authorization code grant but can't protect its secret (i.e. native mobile apps or single-page JavaScript apps), then the client secret is not required when making a request to exchange the auth code for an access token, and PKCE must be used as well. However, some services still do not support PKCE, so it may not be possible to perform an authorization flow from the single-page app itself, and the client-side JavaScript code may need to have a companion server-side component that performs the OAuth flow instead.

Chapter 5
Single-Page Apps

Single-page apps (also known as browser-based apps) run entirely in the browser after loading the JavaScript and HTML source code from a web page. Since the entire source is available to the browser, they cannot maintain the confidentiality of a client secret, so a secret is not used for these apps. Because they can't use a client secret, the best option is to use the PKCE extension to protect the authorization code in the redirect. This is similar to the solution for mobile apps which also can't use a client secret.

Figure 5-1 illustrates an example where the user interacts with their browser, which in turn makes API requests directly to the service. After first downloading the Javascript and HTML source code from the client, the browser then makes direct API requests to the service. In this case, the app's server never makes API requests to the service, since everything is handled directly in the browser.

Deprecation Notice

A common historical pattern for single-page apps was to use the Implicit flow to receive an access token in the redirect without the intermediate authorization code exchange step. This has a number of security issues as described on page 61 and should no longer be used. Please see https://oauth.net/2/browser-based-apps/ for more details.

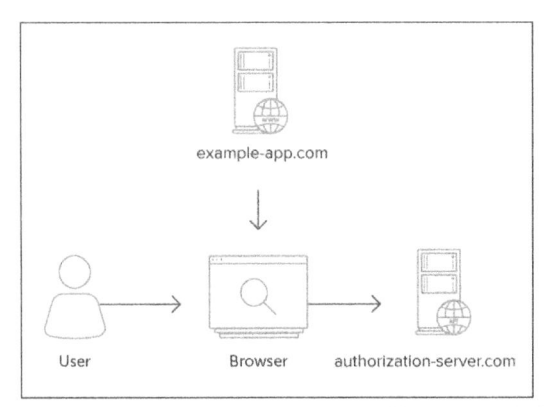

Figure 5-1: The user's browser communicates directly with the API server

Authorization

The authorization code is a temporary code that the client will exchange for an access token. The code itself is obtained from the authorization server where the user gets a chance to see what the information the client is requesting, and approve or deny the request.

The first step of the flow is to request authorization from the user. This is accomplished by creating an authorization request link for the user to click on.

The client first creates what is known as a PKCE "*code verifier*". This is a cryptographically random string using the characters A-Z, a-z, 0-9, and the punctuation characters -._~ (hyphen, period, underscore, and tilde), between 43 and 128 characters long.

The code verifier needs to be stored somewhere local that the app can look up again when the user is redirected back to the app. In the case of single-page apps, this will typically be a storage API provided by the browser such as LocalStorage.

Once the app has generated the code verifier, it uses that to create the *code challenge*. For devices that can perform a SHA256 hash, the code challenge is a Base64-URL-encoded string of the SHA256 hash of the code verifier. Clients that do not have the ability to perform a SHA256 hash are permitted to use the code verifier string itself as the challenge (aka the `plain` hash method), although it is less secure. This hashed value is sent in the authorization request, so that the original random string is never exposed to anything outside the app.

The authorization request parameters are used to create the authorization URL, such as:

```
https://authorization-server.com/oauth/authorize
  ?client_id=a17c21ed
  &response_type=code
  &state=5ca75bd30
  &redirect_uri=https%3A%2F%2Fexample-app.com%2Fauth
  &scope=photos
  &code_challenge=hKpKupTM391pE10xfQiorMxXarRKAHRhTfH_xkGf7U4
  &code_challenge_method=S256
```

After the user visits the authorization page, the service shows the user an explanation of the request, including application name, scope, etc. If the user clicks "approve", the server will redirect back to the website, with an authorization code and the state value in the URL query string.

Authorization Request Parameters

The following parameters are used to make the authorization request.

response_type=code

`response_type` is set to `code` indicating that you want an authorization code as the response.

client_id

The `client_id` is the identifier for your app. You will have received a client_id when first registering your app with the service.

redirect_uri

The `redirect_uri` is optional in the spec, but some services require it. This is the URL to which you want the user to be redirected after the authorization is complete. This must match the redirect URL that you have previously registered with the service.

scope (optional)

Include one or more scope values to request additional levels of access. The values will depend on the particular service.

state

The `state` parameter serves two functions. When the user is redirected back to your app, whatever value you include as the state will also be included in the redirect. This gives your app a chance to persist data between the user being directed to the authorization server and back again, such as using the state parameter as a session key. This may be used to indicate what action in the app to perform after authorization is complete, for example, indicating which of your app's pages to redirect to after authorization. This also serves as a CSRF protection mechanism.

code_challenge

The Base64-urlencoded hash of the randomly generated secret. See Sample JavaScript Code on page 59 for an example of how to generate this hashed value.

code_challenge_method

A string indicating which hashing method was used to create the code challenge, typically "S256". If no hash was used, and the code challenge is the same as the code verifier, then the value is "plain". This is less secure, but was left in the spec to support devices that are unable to compute a SHA256 hash.

Example Flow

The following step-by-step example illustrates using the authorization code flow for single-page apps.

The app initiates the authorization request

The app initiates the flow by crafting a URL containing the necessary parameters described above. The app can put this into an `<a href="">` tag.

```
<a href="https://authorization-server.com/oauth/authorize
  ?response_type=code&client_id=mRkZGFjM&state=TY2OTZhZGFk
  &scope=photos&code_challenge_method=S256
  &code_challenge=hKpKupTM391pE10xfQiorMxXarRKAHRhTfH_xkGf7U4">
  Connect Your Account</a>
```

The user approves the request

Upon being directed to the authorization server, the user sees the authorization request shown in Figure 5-2.

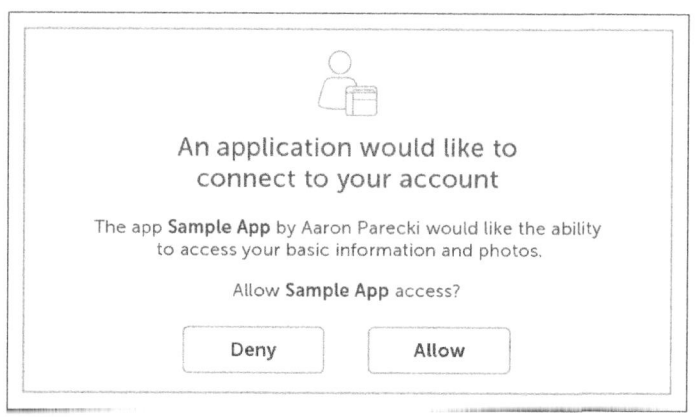

Figure 5-2: Example Authorization Request

After the user is taken to the service and sees the request, they will either allow or deny the request. If they allow the request, they will be redirected back to the redirect URL specified along with an authorization code in the query string. The app then needs to exchange this authorization code for an access token.

```
https://example-app.com/cb?code=Yzk5ZDczMzRlNDEwY
    &state=TY2OTZhZGFk
```

If you include a "state" parameter in the initial authorization URL, the service will return it to you after the user authorizes your app. Your app should compare the state with the state it created in the initial request. This helps ensure that you only exchange authorization codes that you requested, preventing attackers from redirecting to your callback URL with arbitrary or stolen authorization codes.

Exchange the authorization code for an access token

To exchange the authorization code for an access token, the app makes a POST request to the service's token endpoint. The request will have the following parameters.

grant_type (required)

The `grant_type` parameter must be set to "authorization_code".

code (required)

This parameter is for the authorization code received from the authorization server which will be in the query string parameter "code" in this request.

redirect_uri (possibly required)

If the redirect URL was included in the initial authorization request, it must be included in the token request as well, and must be identical. Some services support registering multiple redirect URLs, and some require the redirect URL to be specified on each request. Check the service's documentation for the specifics.

code_verifier (required)

Since the client included a `code_challenge` parameter in the initial request, it must now prove it has the secret used to generate the hash by sending it in the POST request. This is the plaintext string that was used to calculate the hash that was previously sent in the `code_challenge` parameter.

Client Identification (required)

Despite the client secret not being used in this flow, the request requires sending the client ID to identify the application making the request. This means the client must include the client ID as a POST body parameter rather than using HTTP Basic Authentication like it can when including the client secret as well.

```
POST /oauth/token HTTP/1.1
Host: authorization-endpoint.com

grant_type=code
&code=Yzk5ZDczMzRlNDEwY
&redirect_uri=https://example-app.com/cb
&client_id=mRkZGFjM
&code_verifier=Th7UHJdLswIYQxwSg29DbK1a_d9o41uNMTRmuH0PM8zyoMAQ
```

Sample JavaScript Code

Before modern browser APIs, it used to be challenging to generate secure random strings or perform hashing functions without bringing in large libraries. Thankfully, browser APIs have improved with the introduction of things like WebCrypto, and there are now good ways to do the operations necessary for PKCE in plain JavaScript.

Below are some helper functions you might find useful when implementing PKCE in a JavaScript application from scratch.

Generate a Random String

```
// Generate a secure random string using the browser crypto functions
```

```
function generateRandomString() {
  var array = new Uint32Array(28);
  window.crypto.getRandomValues(array);
  return Array.from(array, dec =>
    ('0' + dec.toString(16)).substr(-2)).join('');
}
```

Calculate a SHA256 Hash

```
// Calculate the SHA256 hash of the input text.
// Returns a promise that resolves to an ArrayBuffer
function sha256(plain) {
  const encoder = new TextEncoder();
  const data = encoder.encode(plain);
  return window.crypto.subtle.digest('SHA-256', data);
}
```

Base64 URL Encoding

```
// Base64-URL-Encodes the input string
function base64urlencode(str) {
  // Convert the ArrayBuffer to string using Uint8 array to
  // convert to what btoa accepts. btoa accepts chars only
  // within ascii 0-255 and base64 encodes them.
  // Then convert the base64 encoded to base64url encoded
  //   (replace + with -, replace / with _, trim trailing =)
  return btoa(String.fromCharCode.apply(null, new Uint8Array(str)))
    .replace(/\+/g, '-').replace(/\//g, '_').replace(/=+$/, '');
}
```

Generate the PKCE Challenge

```
// Return the Base64-URL-Encoded SHA256 hash from the plaintext
async function pkceChallengeFromVerifier(v) {
  hashed = await sha256(v);
  return base64urlencode(hashed);
}
```

Hopefully this illustrates that it doesn't require a huge amount of code to support PKCE in JavaScript applications.

Implicit Flow

Some services have historically used the alternative Implicit Flow for single-page apps, rather than the current recommendation of using the Authorization Code with PKCE.

The Implicit Flow bypasses the code exchange step, and instead the access token is returned in the URL fragment to the client immediately.

There are a number of concerns with this approach, enough that many providers have opted to avoid implementing the Implicit flow completely.

The Implicit flow in OAuth 2.0 was created over 10 years ago, when browsers worked very differently than they do today. The primary reason the Implicit flow was created was because of an old limitation in browsers. It used to be the case that JavaScript could only make requests to the same domain that the page was loaded from. However, the standard OAuth Authorization Code flow requires that a POST request is made to the OAuth server's token endpoint, which is often on a different domain than the app. That meant there was previously no way to use this flow from JavaScript. The Implicit flow worked around this limitation by avoiding that POST request, and instead returning the access token immediately in the redirect.

Today, Cross-Origin Resource Sharing (CORS) is universally adopted by browsers, removing the need for this compromise. CORS provides a way for JavaScript to make requests to servers on a different domain as long as the destination allows it. This opens up the possibility of using the Authorization Code flow in JavaScript.

It's worth noting that the Implicit flow has always been seen as a compromise compared to the Authorization Code flow. For example, the spec provides no mechanism to return a refresh token in the Implicit flow, as it was seen as too insecure to allow that. The spec also recommends short lifetimes and limited scope for access tokens issued via the Implicit flow.

In any case, with both the Implicit Flow as well as the Authorization Code Flow with PKCE, the server must require registration of the redirect URL in order to maintain the security of the flow.

Security Considerations

With browser-based apps there is always a risk of things like Cross-Site Scripting (XSS) attacks due to the increased attack surface and number of moving parts in websites. Additionally, browsers currently don't have a secure storage mechanism available to store things like the access token or refresh token. As such, browsers are always considered a higher risk in an OAuth deployment compared to other platforms, and the authorization server will usually have special policies around token lifetimes to mitigate that risk.

Refresh Tokens

Historically, with the Implicit flow, there was never any mechanism for returning refresh tokens to JavaScript applications. This made sense at the time, because it was well known that the Implicit flow was less secure, and without a client secret, a refresh token can be used to get new access tokens indefinitely, so this would be an even greater risk than a leaked access token. There was also little need for a refresh token since JavaScript apps would only be running when the user was actively using the browser, so they could redirect to the authorization server to get a new access token if needed.

With the developments over the last few years of adopting PKCE for JavaScript apps, there is now the potential for refresh tokens to be issued to JavaScript apps as well. This ends up being a policy decision of the authorization server as to whether refresh tokens will be issued, depending on the level of risk the authorization server is willing to tolerate.

Additionally, the additions of browser APIs such as `ServiceWorkers` means that now browser-based apps have the potential to run code when the user isn't actively using the browser, such as in response to a Background Sync event. This means there is now more potential use for refresh tokens in browser apps.

If the authorization server wishes to allow JavaScript apps to use refresh tokens, then they must also follow the best practices outlined in "OAuth 2.0 Security Best Current Practice (https://datatracker.ietf.org/doc/html/draft-ietf-oauth-security-topics)" and "OAuth 2.0 for Browser-Based Apps (https://datatracker.ietf.org/doc/html/draft-ietf-oauth-browser-based-apps)", two recent documents adopted by the OAuth Working Group. Specifically, refresh tokens must be valid for only one use, and the authorization server must issue a new refresh token each time a new access token is issued in response to a refresh token grant. This provides the authorization server a way to detect if a refresh token has been copied and used by an attacker, since in normal operation of an app a refresh token would be used only once.

Refresh tokens must also either have a set maximum lifetime, or expire if they are not used within some amount of time. This is again another way to help mitigate the risks of a stolen refresh token.

Storing Tokens

The browser-based app will need to temporarily store some pieces of information during the authorization flow, and then permanently store the resulting access token and refresh token. This provides some challenges in the browser environment since there are currently no general-purpose secure storage mechanism in browsers.

Generally, the browser's `LocalStorage` API is the best place to store this data as it provides the easiest API to store and retrieve data and is about as secure as you can get in a browser. The downside is that any scripts on the page, even from different domains such as your analytics or ad network, will be able to access the `LocalStorage` of your application. This means anything you store in `LocalStorage` is potentially visible to third-party scripts on your page.

Because of the risks of data leakage from third-party scripts, it is extremely important to have a good Content-Security Policy configured for your app so that you can be more confident that arbitrary scripts aren't able to run in the application. A good document on configuring a Content Security Policy is available from OWASP at *https://owasp.org/www-project-cheat-sheets/cheatsheets/Content_Security_Policy_Cheat_Sheet.html*

Choosing an Alternative Architecture

Due to the inherent risks of performing an OAuth flow in a pure JavaScript environment, as well as the risks of storing tokens in a JavaScript app, it is also advisable to consider an alternative architecture where the OAuth flow is handled outside of the JavaScript code by a dynamic backend component. This is a relatively common architectural pattern where an application is served from a dynamic backend such as a .NET or Java app, but it uses a single-page app framework like React or Angular for its UI. If your app falls under this architectural pattern, then the best option is to move all of the OAuth flow to the server component, and keep the access tokens and refresh tokens out of the browser entirely. Note that in this case since your app has a dynamic backend, it is also considered a confidential client and can use a client secret to further protect the OAuth exchanges.

This pattern is described in more detail in "OAuth 2.0 for Browser-Based Apps *(https://datatracker.ietf.org/doc/html/draft-ietf-oauth-browser-based-apps)*".

Chapter 6
Mobile and Native Apps

Like single-page apps, mobile apps also cannot maintain the confidentiality of a client secret. Because of this, mobile apps must also use an OAuth flow that does not require a client secret. The current best practice is to use the Authorization Flow with PKCE, along with launching an external browser, in order to ensure the native app cannot modify the browser window or inspect the contents.

Many websites provide mobile SDKs which handle the authorization process for you. For those services, you are probably better off using their SDKs directly, since they may have augmented their APIs with non-standard additions. Google provides an open source library called AppAuth which handles the implementation details of the flow described below. It is meant to be able to work with any OAuth 2.0 server that implements the spec. In the case that the service does not a provide their own abstraction, and you have to use their OAuth 2.0 endpoints directly, this section describes how to use the authorization code flow with PKCE to interface with an API.

Authorization

Create a "Log in" button that will open a secure web browser within the app (`ASWebAuthenticationSession` or `SFSafariViewController` on iOS, and "Custom Tabs" on Android). You'll use the same parameters for the authorization request as described in Server-Side Apps on page 41 including the PKCE parameters.

The resulting redirect will include the temporary authorization code which the app will exchange for an access token from its native code.

Example

In this example we will walk through a simple iPhone application that obtains authorization to access a fictional API.

Initiate the authorization request

To begin the authorization process, the app should have a "sign in" button. The link should be constructed as a full URL to the service's authorization endpoint.

The client first creates what is known as a PKCE "*code verifier*". This is a cryptographically random string using the characters `A-Z`, `a-z`, `0-9`, and the punctuation characters `-._~` (hyphen, period, underscore, and tilde), between 43 and 128 characters long.

Once the app has generated the code verifier, it uses that to create the *code challenge*. The code challenge is a Base64-URL-encoded string of the SHA256 hash of the code verifier. This hashed value is sent in the authorization request, so that the original random string is never exposed to anything outside the app.

The authorization request parameters are used to create the authorization URL, such as:

```
https://authorization-server.com/authorize
  ?client_id=eKNjzFFjH9A1ysYd
  &response_type=code
  &redirect_uri=com.example.app://auth
  &state=1234zyx
  &scope=photos
  &code_challenge=hKpKupTM381pE10yfQiorMxXarRKAHRhTfH_xkGf7U4
  &code_challenge_method=S256
```

Note in this case the custom scheme of the redirect URL. Both iOS and Android provide the ability for apps to register custom URL schemes which can be used as the redirect URL. This is also sometimes called "deep linking" in the platform's documentation. Both platforms also allow the app to register itself to be launched when a matching URL pattern is visited ("Universal Links" on iOS and "App Links" on Android). Both methods provide approximately the same experience when using an app, but the "Universal/App Links" method provides better fallback behavior when the URL is visited if the user doesn't have the app installed. The "Universal Links" and "App Links" methods are generally considered more modern and are probably what you should use going forward.

When the user taps the "Sign In" button, the app should open the authorization URL in a secure in-app browser (ASWebAuthenticationSession on iOS, or a "Custom Tab" on Android). Using an embedded WebView window within the app is considered extremely dangerous, as this provides the user no guarantee they are looking at the service's own website and so is an easy source of a phishing attack. The embedded web view also provides a worse user experience since it does not share system cookies and the user will always have to enter their credentials. By using the platform's secure browser APIs which share cookies with the system browser, you have the advantage of the user potentially already being signed in to the service as well and not needing to enter their credentials every time.

The user approves the request

Upon being directed to the authorization server, the user sees an authorization request such as the one shown in Figure 6-1.

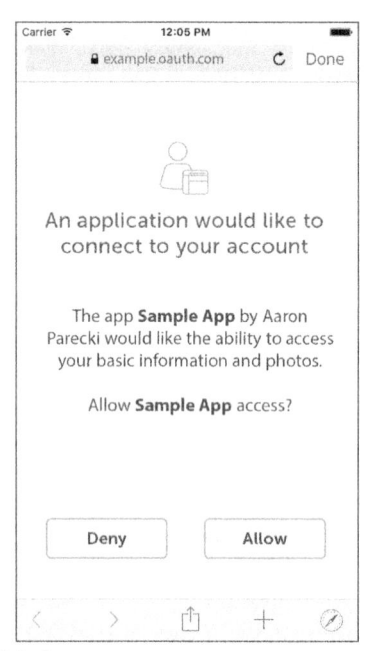

Figure 6-1: An embedded `ASWebAuthenticationSession`. *The "Done" button in the top right corner collapses the view and returns the user to the app.*

The service redirects the user back to the app

When the user finishes signing in, the service will redirect back to your app's redirect URL which will cause the secure browser API to send the resulting URL to your app. The `Location` header from the redirect will look something like the following, which will be passed to your app.

```
com.example.app://auth?state=1234zyx
    &code=lS0KgilpRsT07qT_iMOg9bBSaWqODC1g06gV2GYtyynB6A
```

Your app should then parse out the state value and authorization code from the URL, verify the state matches the value it set, and then exchange the authorization code for an access token.

Exchange the authorization code for an access token

To exchange the authorization code for an access token, the app makes a POST request to the service's token endpoint. This happens from the app's native code rather than from within the browser, since that's where the PKCE code_verifier was stored. The request will have the following parameters.

grant_type (required)

The `grant_type` parameter must be set to "authorization_code".

code (required)

This parameter is for the authorization code received from the authorization server which will be in the query string parameter "code" in this request.

redirect_uri (possibly required)

If the redirect URL was included in the initial authorization request, it must be included in the token request as well, and must be identical. Some services support registering multiple redirect URLs, and some require the redirect URL to be specified on each request. Check the service's documentation for the specifics.

code_verifier (required)

Since the client included a `code_challenge` parameter in the initial request, it must now prove it has the secret used to generate the hash by sending it in the POST request. This is the plaintext string that was used to calculate the hash that was previously sent in the `code_challenge` parameter.

Client Identification (required)

Despite the client secret not being used in this flow, the request requires sending the client ID to identify the application making the request. This means the client must include the client ID as a POST body parameter rather than using HTTP Basic Authentication like it can when including the client secret as well.

```
POST /oauth/token HTTP/1.1
Host: authorization-endpoint.com

grant_type=code
&code=Yzk5ZDczMzRlNDEwY
&redirect_uri=com.example.app://auth
&client_id=eKNjzFFjH9A1ysYd
&code_verifier=Th7UHJdLswIYQxwSg29DbK1a_d9o41uNMTRmuH0PM8zyoMAQ
```

Security Considerations

Always use the secure embedded browser APIs, or launch a native browser

It is critical that the application use the appropriate browser APIs on the platforms rather than use embedded web views. On iOS, this is either `ASWebAuthenticationSession` or `SFSafariViewController`, and on Android this is known as "Custom Tabs".

Using an embedded web view has many downsides, resulting in a higher likelihood of the user falling for a phishing attack since it provides no way for the user to verify the origin of the web page they're looking at. It would be trivial for an attacker to create a web page that looks just like the authorization web page and embed it in their own malicious app, giving them the ability to steal usernames and passwords.

On the user experience side, using an embedded web view also has the downside of the web view not sharing system cookies so the user will be forced to enter their credentials every time. Instead, using the appropriate secure browser APIs will provide the opportunity for the user to bypass entering their credentials in the app if they're already logged in to the authorization server in their browser.

Chapter 7
Making Authenticated Requests

Regardless of which grant type you used or whether you used a client secret, you now have an OAuth 2.0 Bearer Token you can use with the API.

The access token is sent to the service in the HTTP `Authorization` header prefixed by the text `Bearer`. Historically, some services allowed the token to be sent in the post body parameter or even the GET query string, but there are downsides to these approaches and for the most part modern implementations will use only the HTTP header method.

When passing in the access token in an HTTP header, you should make a request like the following:

```
POST /resource/1/update HTTP/1.1
Authorization: Bearer RsT5OjbzRn430zqMLgV3Ia
Host: api.authorization-server.com

description=Hello+World
```

The access token is not intended to be parsed or understood by your application. The only thing your application should do with it is use it to make API requests. Some services will use structured tokens like JWTs as their access tokens, described in Chapter 12, *Self-Encoded Access Tokens,* but the client does not need to worry about decoding the token in this case.

In fact, attempting to decode the access token is dangerous, as the server makes no guarantees that access tokens will always continue to be in the same format. It's entirely possible that the next time you get an access token from the service, it will be in a different format. The thing to keep in mind is that access tokens are opaque to the client, and should only be used to make API requests and not interpreted themselves.

If you are trying to find out whether your access token has expired, you can either store the expiration lifetime that was returned when you first got the access token, or just try to make the request anyway, and get a new access token if the current one has expired. In practice, there isn't much of a difference. While preemptively refreshing the access token can save an HTTP request, you still need to handle the case when an API call reports an expired token before you were expecting it to expire, since access tokens can expire for many reasons beyond just their expected lifetime.

See below for more details on getting new access tokens using refresh tokens.

If you're trying to find out more information about the user who signed in, you should read the API docs of the particular service to find out their recommendation. For example, Google's API uses OpenID Connect to provide a userinfo endpoint that can return info about the user given an access token, or you can get the user's information from an ID token instead. We walk through a complete example of the userinfo endpoint workflow in Chapter 3, *Signing in with Google*.

Refresh Tokens

When you initially received the access token, it may have included a refresh token as well as an expiration time like in the example below.

```
{
  "access_token": "AYjcyMzY3ZDhiNmJkNTY",
  "refresh_token": "RjY2NjM5NzA2OWJjuE7c",
  "token_type": "Bearer",
  "expires_in": 3600
}
```

The presence of the refresh token means that the access token will expire and you'll be able to get a new one without the user's interaction.

The "expires_in" value is the number of seconds that the access token will be valid. It's up to the service you're using to decide how long access tokens will be valid, and may depend on the application or the organization's own policies. You could use this timestamp to preemptively refresh your access tokens instead of waiting for a request with an expired token to fail. Some people like to get a new access token shortly before the current one will expire in order to save an HTTP request of an API call failing. While that is a perfectly fine optimization, it doesn't stop you from still needing to handle the case where an API call fails if an access token expires before the expected time. Access tokens can expire for many reasons, such as the user revoking an app, or if the authorization server expires all tokens when a user changes their password.

If you make an API request and the token has expired already, you'll get back a response indicating as such. You can check for this specific error code, and then refresh the token and try the request again.

If you're using a JSON-based API, then it will likely return a JSON error response with the `invalid_token` error. In any case, the `WWW-Authenticate` header will also have the `invalid_token` error code.

```
HTTP/1.1 401 Unauthorized
WWW-Authenticate: Bearer error="invalid_token"
  error_description="The access token expired"
Content-type: application/json

{
  "error": "invalid_token",
  "error_description": "The access token expired"
}
```

When your application recognizes this specific error, it can then make a request to the token endpoint using the refresh token it previously received, and will get back a new access token it can use to retry the original request.

To use the refresh token, make a POST request to the service's token endpoint with `grant_type=refresh_token`, and include the refresh token as well as the client credentials if required.

```
POST /oauth/token HTTP/1.1
Host: authorization-server.com

grant_type=refresh_token
&refresh_token=xxxxxxxxxxx
&client_id=xxxxxxxxxx
&client_secret=xxxxxxxxxx
```

The response will be a new access token, and may contain a new refresh token, just like you received when exchanging the authorization code for an access token.

```
{
  "access_token": "BWjcyMzY3ZDhiNmJkNTY",
  "refresh_token": "Srq2NjM5NzA2OWJjuE7c",
  "token_type": "Bearer",
  "expires_in": 3600
}
```

If you do not get back a new refresh token, then it means your existing refresh token will continue to work when the new access token expires.

The most secure option is for the authorization server to issue a new refresh token each time one is used. This is the recommendation in the latest *Security Best Current Practice (https://datatracker.ietf.org/doc/html/draft-ietf-oauth-security-topics)* which enables authorization servers to detect if a refresh token is stolen. This is especially important for clients that don't have a client secret, since the refresh token becomes the only thing needed to get new access tokens.

When the refresh token changes after each use, if the authorization server ever detects a refresh token was used twice, it means it has likely been copied and is being used by an attacker, and the authorization server can revoke all access tokens and refresh tokens associated with it immediately.

Keep in mind that at any point the user can revoke an application (page 153), so your application needs to be able to handle the case when using the refresh token also fails. At that point, you will need to prompt the user for authorization again, beginning a new OAuth flow from scratch.

You might notice that the "expires_in" property refers to the access token, not the refresh token. The expiration time of the refresh token is intentionally never communicated to the client. This is because the client has no actionable steps it can take even if it were able to know when the refresh token would expire. There are also many reasons refresh tokens may expire prior to any expected lifetime of them as well.

If a refresh token expires for any reason, then the only action the application can take is to ask the user to log in again, starting a new OAuth flow from scratch, which will issue a new access token and refresh token to the application. That's the reason it doesn't matter whether the application knows the expected lifetime of the refresh token, because regardless of the reason it expires the outcome is always the same.

Chapter 7: Making Authenticated Requests

Part II
Building an OAuth 2.0 Server

Chapter 8
Client Registration

Registering a New Application

When a developer comes to your website, they will need a way to create a new application and obtain credentials for it. Typically you will have them create a developer account (or create an account on behalf of their organization) before they can create an application.

While the OAuth 2.0 spec doesn't require you to collect any particular application information before granting application credentials, most services collect basic information about an app, such as the app name and an icon, before issuing the `client_id` and `client_secret`. It is, however, important that you require the developer to register one or more redirect URLs for the application for security purposes. This is explained in more detail in Chapter 11, *Redirect URLs*.

Typically services collect information about an application such as:

- Application name
- An icon for the application
- URL to the application's home page
- A short description of the application
- A link to the application's privacy policy
- A list of redirect URLs

Figure 8-1 shows GitHub's interface for registering an application. In it, they collect the application name, home page URL, the callback URL, and an optional description.

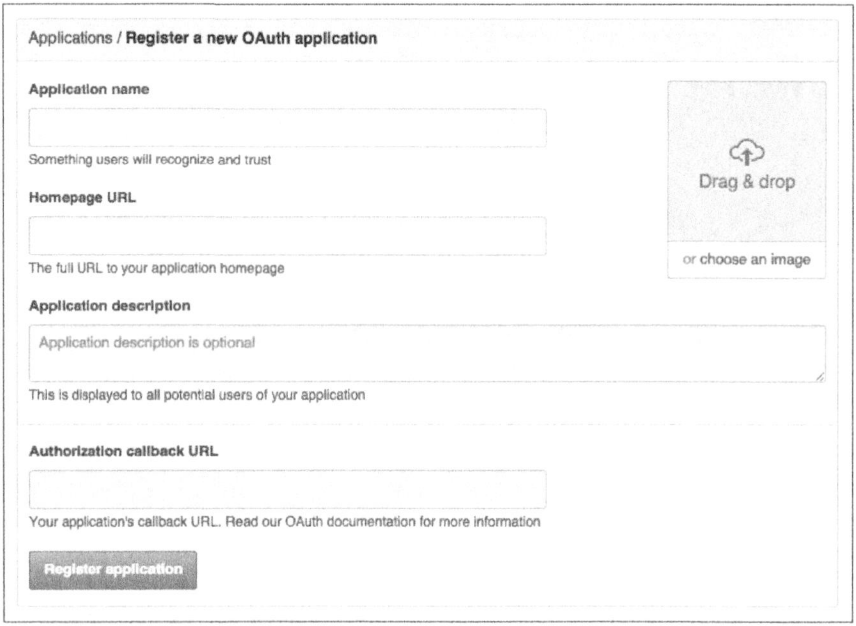

Figure 8-1: GitHub's application creation interface

It is a good idea to specify to your developers whether the information you are collecting from them will be displayed to end users, or whether it is for internal use only.

Foursquare's application registration page shown in Figure 8-2 asks for similar information, but they additionally ask for a short tagline and a privacy policy URL. These are displayed to the user in the authorization prompt.

Due to the security considerations with using the legacy Implicit grant type, some services (such as Instagram) disable this grant type for new applications by default, and require that the developer explicitly enables it in the application's settings, as shown in Figure 8-3.

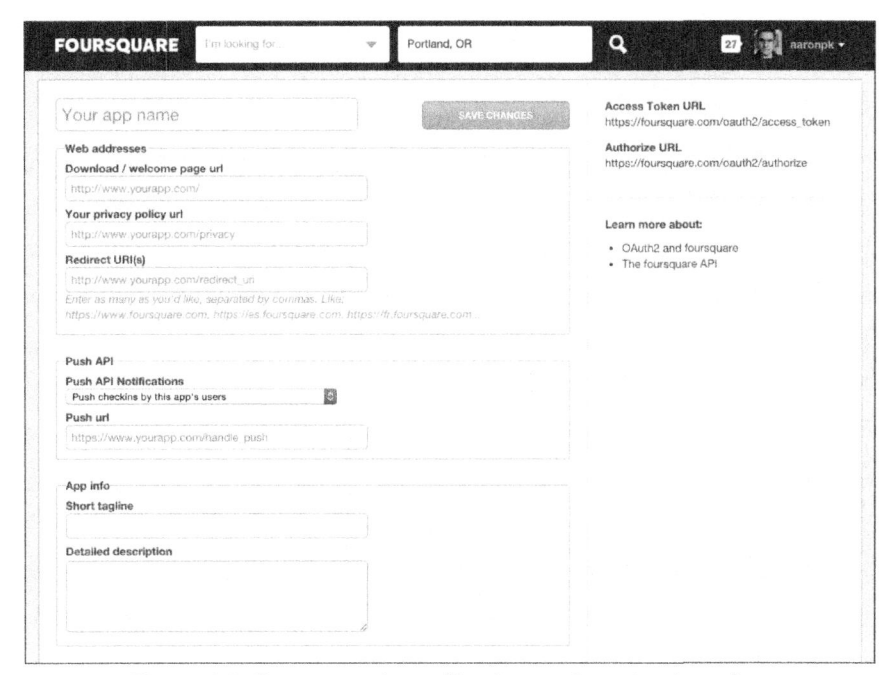

Figure 8-2: Foursquare's application registration interface

Instagram provides a note instructing developers to not name their applications with words that might make the app appear to be from Instagram. This is also a good place to include a link to the API Terms of Use.

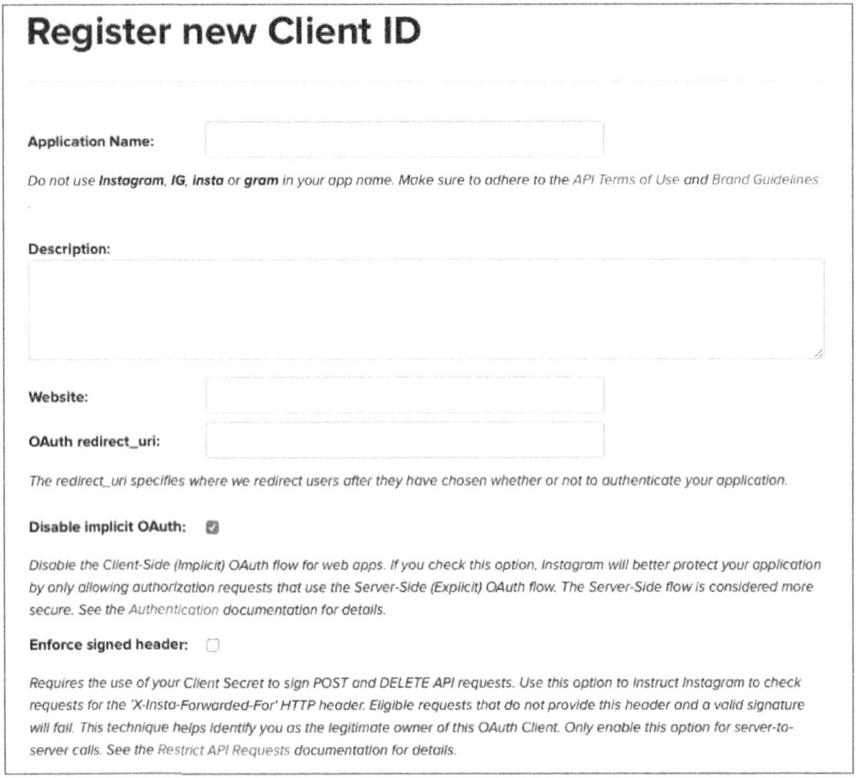

Register new Client ID

Application Name:

Do not use *Instagram*, *IG*, *insta* or *gram* in your app name. Make sure to adhere to the API Terms of Use and Brand Guidelines

Description:

Website:

OAuth redirect_uri:

The redirect_uri specifies where we redirect users after they have chosen whether or not to authenticate your application.

Disable implicit OAuth: ☑

Disable the Client-Side (Implicit) OAuth flow for web apps. If you check this option, Instagram will better protect your application by only allowing authorization requests that use the Server-Side (Explicit) OAuth flow. The Server-Side flow is considered more secure. See the Authentication documentation for details.

Enforce signed header: ☐

Requires the use of your Client Secret to sign POST and DELETE API requests. Use this option to instruct Instagram to check requests for the 'X-Insta-Forwarded-For' HTTP header. Eligible requests that do not provide this header and a valid signature will fail. This technique helps identify you as the legitimate owner of this OAuth Client. Only enable this option for server-to-server calls. See the Restrict API Requests documentation for details.

Figure 8-3: Instagram's application registration interface

Your service can also make the developer choose the type of application they are creating, (public or confidential), or choose a description of the app platform which may be more relatable to the developer (web app, mobile app, SPA, etc). Your service should only issue a client secret to confidential applications, and disallow use of the Implicit grant for those applications as well.

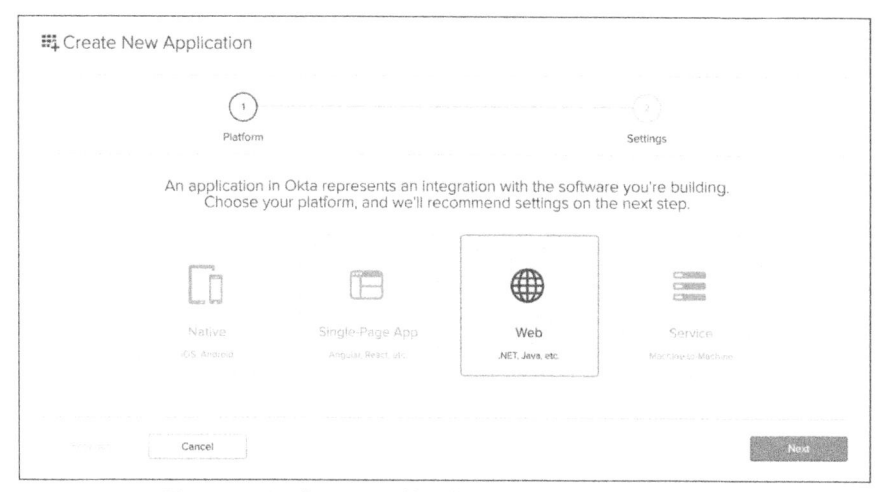

Figure 8-4: Okta's application registration interface

As shown in Figure 8-4, Okta lets the developer choose which platform the application is for (Native, Single-Page App, Web, or Service) before collecting information about the app. Depending on the value the developer chooses here, that will determine things like which grant types are enabled for the app, and whether the app is issued a client secret.

The Client ID and Secret

At this point, you've built the application registration screen, you're ready to let the developer register the application. When the developer registers the application, you'll need to generate a client ID and optionally a secret. When generating these strings, there are some important things to consider in terms of security and aesthetics.

Client ID

The `client_id` is a public identifier for apps. Even though it's public, it's best that it isn't guessable by third parties, so many implementations use something like a 32-character hex string. If the client ID is guessable, it makes it slightly easier to craft phishing attacks against arbitrary applications. It must also be unique across all clients that the authorization server handles.

Here are some examples of client IDs from services that support OAuth 2.0:

- Foursquare: `ZYDPLLBWSK3MVQJSIYHB1OR2JXCY0X2C5UJ2QAR2MAAIT5Q`
- GitHub: `6779ef20e75817b79602`
- Google: `292085223830.apps.googleusercontent.com`
- Instagram: `f2a1ed52710d4533bde25be6da03b6e3`
- SoundCloud: `269d98e4922fb3895e9ae2108cbb5064`
- Windows Live: `00000000400ECB04`
- Okta: `0oa2hl2inow5Uqc6c357`

If the developer is creating a "public" app (a mobile or single-page app), then you should not issue a `client_secret` to the app at all. This is the only way to ensure the developer won't accidentally include it in their application. If it doesn't exist, it can't be leaked!

Because of this, it's usually a good idea to ask the developer what type of application they are creating when they start. You can present the following options to them, and only issue a secret for "web server" or "service" apps.

- Web-server app
- Single-page app
- Mobile or native app
- Service app

Of course there's nothing stopping the developer from choosing the wrong option, but by taking the initiative of asking the developer what kind of app the credentials will be used by, you can help reduce the likelihood of leaked secrets.

Client Secret

The `client_secret` is a secret known only to the application and the authorization server. It is essential the application's own password. It must be sufficiently random to not be guessable, which means you should avoid using common UUID libraries which often take into account the timestamp or MAC address of the server generating it. A great way to generate a secure secret is to use a cryptographically-secure library to generate a 256-bit value and then convert it to a hexadecimal representation.

In PHP, you can use the `random_bytes` function and convert to a hex string:

```
bin2hex(random_bytes(32));
```

In Ruby, you can use the SecureRandom library to generate a hex string:

```
require 'securerandom'
SecureRandom.hex(32)
```

It is critical that developers never include their `client_secret` in public (mobile or browser-based) clients. To help developers avoid accidentally doing this, it's best to make the client secret visually different from the ID. This way when developers copy and paste the ID and secret, it is easy to recognize which is which. Usually using a longer string for the secret is a good way to indicate this, or prefixing the secret with "secret" or "private".

Storing and Displaying the Client ID and Secret

For each registered application, you'll need to store the public `client_id` and the private `client_secret`. Because these are essentially equivalent to a username and password, you should not store the secret in plain text, instead only store an encrypted or hashed version, to help reduce the likelihood of the secret leaking.

When you issue the client ID and secret, you will need to display them to the developer. Most services provide a way for developers to retrieve the secret of an existing application, although some will only display the secret one time and require the developer store it themselves immediately. If you display the secret only one time, you can store a hashed version of it to avoid storing the plaintext secret at all.

If you store the secret in a way that can be displayed later to developers, you should take extra precautions when revealing the secret. A common way to protect the secret is to insert a "re-authorization" prompt before the developer can view the secret.

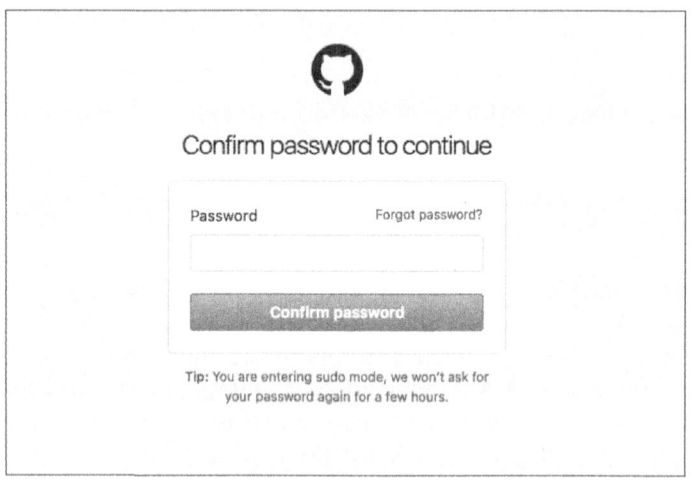

Figure 8-5: GitHub prompts for your password when making sensitive changes or viewing the application's secret

The service asks the developer to confirm their password before it will reveal the secret. This is commonly seen in Amazon or GitHub's websites when you attempt to view or update sensitive information.

Chapter 8: Client Registration

App key	53geej95rk20660
App secret	Show

Figure 8-6: Dropbox hides the secret until it is clicked

Additionally, obscuring the secret on the application detail page until the developer clicks "show" is a good way to prevent accidental leakage of the secret.

Deleting Applications and Revoking Secrets

Developers will need a way to delete (or at least deactivate) their applications. It is also a good idea to provide a way for the developer to revoke and generate a new client secret for their apps.

Deleting Applications

When the developer deletes an application, the service should inform the developer about the consequences of deleting the application. For example, GitHub tells the developer that all access tokens will be revoked, and how many users will be affected.

Deleting an application should immediately revoke all access tokens and other credentials that were issued to the application such as pending authorization codes and refresh tokens.

Figure 8-7: GitHub asks to confirm deleting an application

Revoking Secrets

The service should provide the developer with a way to reset the client secret. In the case when the secret is accidentally exposed, the developer needs a way to ensure the old secret can be revoked. Revoking the secret should not necessarily invalidate users' access tokens, since the developer could always delete the application if they wanted to also invalidate all user tokens.

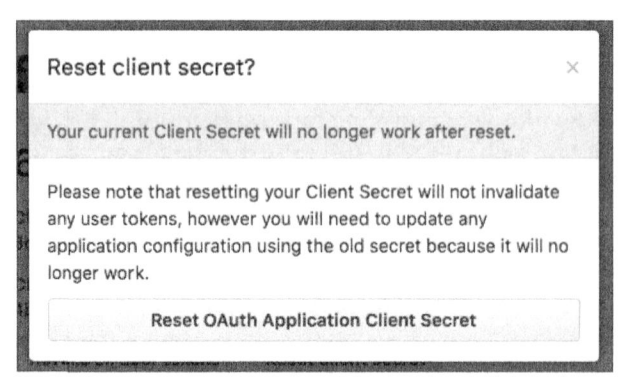

Figure 8-8: GitHub asks to confirm resetting an application's secret

Resetting the secret should keep all existing access tokens active. However this does mean that any deployed applications using the old secret will be unable to refresh the access token using the old secret. The deployed applications will need to update their secrets before they will be able to use a refresh token.

Chapter 9
Authorization

The authorization interface is the screen users see when granting applications access to their account. The following sections cover how to build the authorization screen, what components to include in the interface, and how best to present the interface to end users.

When implementing an OAuth server, you are enabling a developer community to build applications that leverage your platform, allowing applications to access and potentially modify private user content, or act on behalf of users. Because of this, you need to ensure you are empowering your users with as much information as possible to protect their accounts and ensure they are informed as to what applications are doing with their accounts.

The Authorization Request

Clients will direct a user's browser to the authorization server to begin the OAuth process. Along with the type of grant specified by the `response_type` parameter, the request will have a number of other parameters to indicate the specifics of the request.

Chapter 4, *Server-Side Apps,* describes how clients will build the authorization URL for your service. The first time the authorization server sees the user will be this authorization request, the user will be directed to the server with the query parameters the client has set. At this point, the authorization server will need to validate the request and present the authorization interface, allowing the user to approve or deny the request.

Request Parameters

The following parameters are used to begin the authorization request. For example, if the authorization server URL is `https://authorization-server.com/auth` then the client will craft a URL like the following and direct the user's browser to it:

```
https://authorization-server.com/auth?response_type=code
&client_id=29352735982374239857
&redirect_uri=https://example-app.com/callback
&scope=create+delete
&state=xcoivjuywkdkhvusuye3kch
```

response_type

`response_type` will be set to `code`, indicating that the application expects to receive an authorization code if successful.

client_id

The `client_id` is the public identifier for the app.

redirect_uri (optional)

The `redirect_uri` is not required by the spec, but your service should require it. This URL must match one of the URLs the developer registered when creating the application, and the authorization server should reject the request if it does not match.

scope (optional)

The request may have one or more scope values indicating additional access requested by the application. The authorization server will need to display the requested scopes in a way that is meaningful to the end user.

state (recommended)

The `state` parameter is used by the application to store request-specific data and/or prevent CSRF attacks. The authorization server must return the unmodified state value back to the application.

PKCE

If the authorization server supports the PKCE extension (described in Chapter 17, *PKCE*,) then the `code_challenge` and `code_challenge_method` parameters will also be present. These must be remembered by the authorization server between issuing the authorization code and issuing the access token.

Verifying the Authorization Request

The authorization server must first verify that the `client_id` in the request corresponds to a valid application.

If your server allows applications to register more than one redirect URL, then there are two steps to validating the redirect URL. If the request contains a `redirect_uri` parameter, the server must confirm it is a valid redirect URL for this application. If there is no `redirect_uri` parameter in the request, and only one URL was registered, the server uses the redirect URL that was previously registered. Otherwise, if no redirect URL is in the request, and no redirect URL has been registered, this is an error.

If the `client_id` is invalid, the server should reject the request immediately and display the error to the user rather than redirecting the user back to the application.

Invalid Redirect URL

If the authorization server detects a problem with the redirect URL, it needs to inform the user of the problem instead of redirecting the user. The redirect URL could be invalid for a number of reasons, including:

- the redirect URL parameter is missing
- the redirect URL parameter was invalid, such as if it was a string that does not parse as a URL
- the redirect URL does not match one of the registered redirect URLs for the application

In these cases, the authorization server should display an error to the user informing them of the problem. The server must not redirect the user back to the application. This avoids what is known as an "open redirector" attack. (*https://oauth.net/advisories/ 2014-1-covert-redirect/*) The server should only redirect the user to the redirect URL if the redirect URL is an exact match of a registered redirect URL.

Other Errors

All other errors should be handled by redirecting the user to the redirect URL with an error code in the query string. See Authorization Response on page 99 for details on how to respond with an error.

If the request is missing the `response_type` parameter, or the value of that parameter is anything besides `code` or `token` (or a response type defined by an extension), the server can return an `invalid_request` error.

Since the authorization server may require clients to specify if they are public or confidential, it can reject authorization requests that aren't allowed. For example, if the client specified they are a confidential client, the server can reject a request that uses `response_type=token`. When rejecting for this reason, use the error code `unauthorized_client`.

The authorization server should reject the request if there are scope values that it doesn't recognize. In this case, the server can redirect to the callback URL with the `invalid_scope` error code.

The authorization server needs to store the "state" value (and PKCE values) for this request in order to include it in the authorization response. The server must not modify or make any assumptions about what the state value contains, since it is purely for the benefit of the client.

Requiring User Login

The first thing the user will see after clicking the application's "sign in" or "connect" button is your authorization server UI. It's up to the authorization server to decide whether to require the user log in each time they visit the authorization screen, or keep the user signed in for some period of time. If the authorization server remembers the user in between requests, then it may still need to ask the user's permission to authorize the application on future visits.

Typically sites like Twitter or Facebook expect their users are signed in most of the time, so they provide a way for their authorization screens to give the user a streamlined experience by not requiring them to log in each time. However, based on the security requirements of your service as well as that of the third-party applications, it may be desirable to require or give developers the option to require the user to log in each time they visit the authorization screen.

In Google's API, applications can add `prompt=login` to the authorization request, which causes the authorization server to force the user to sign in again before it will show the authorization prompt.

In any case, if the user is signed out, or doesn't yet have an account on your service, you'll need to provide a way for them to sign in or create an account on this screen.

Authenticating the user can be done any way you wish, as this is not specified in the OAuth 2.0 spec. Most services use a traditional username/password login to authenticate their users, but this is by no means the only way you can approach the problem. In enterprise environments, a common technique is to use SAML to leverage an existing authentication mechanism at the organization, while avoiding creating another username/password database.

This is also the opportunity the authorization server has to require multifactor authentication from the user. After authenticating with the user's primary username and password, the authorization server can require a second factor such as WebAuthn or a USB security key. The benefit of this pattern is the applications do not need to be aware of whether multifactor authentication is being used or required, since that happens entirely between the user and the authorization server without being visible to the application.

Once the user authenticates with the authorization server, it can continue to process the authorization request and redirect the user back to the application. Sometimes the server will consider a successful login to also mean that the user authorized the application. In this case, the authorization screen with the login prompt would need to include text that describes the fact that by signing in, the user is approving this authorization request. This would result in the following user flow.

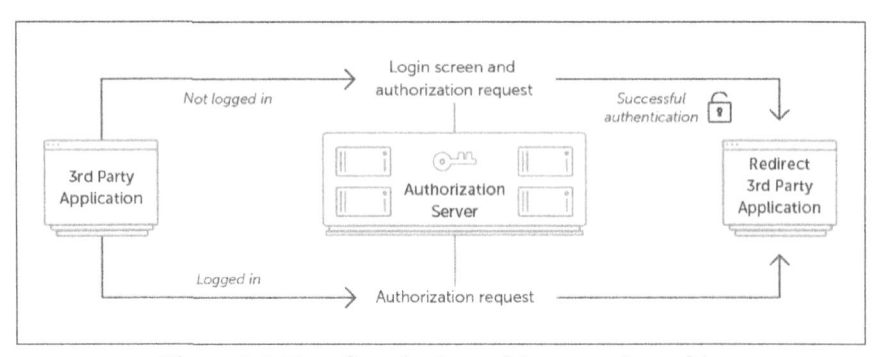

Figure 9-1: User flow for logged-in vs not-logged-in

If the authorization server needs to authenticate the user via SAML or with some other internal system, the user flow would look like the following

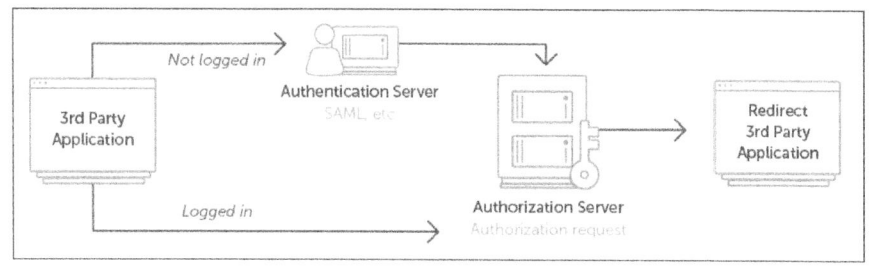

Figure 9-2: User flow for separate authentication server

In this flow, the user is directed back to the authorization server after signing in, where they see the authorization request as they would if they had already been signed in.

The Authorization Interface

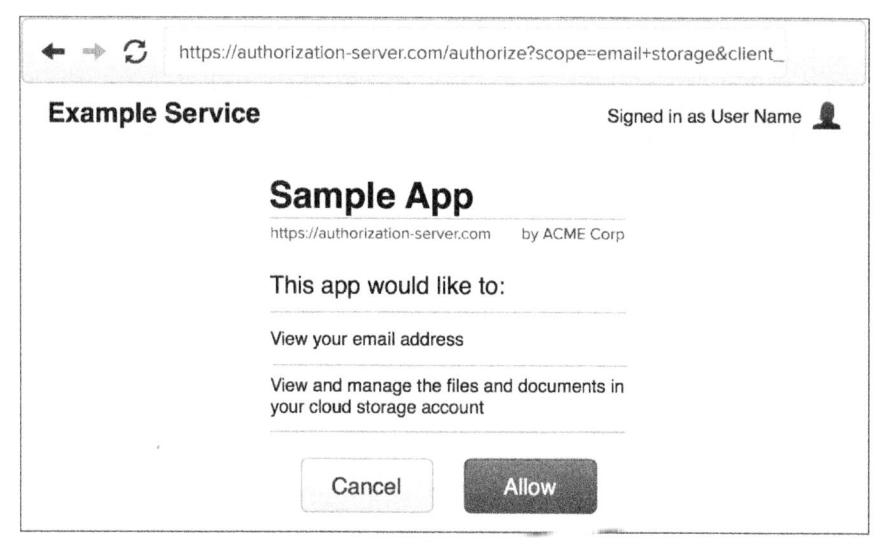

Figure 9-3: Example OAuth Authorization Screen

The authorization interface is the screen users will see when they are presented with an authorization request from a third-party app. This is often also referred to as the "consent screen" or "permission prompt". Since the user is being asked to grant some level of access to a third-party app, you need to ensure the user has all the information they need to make an informed decision about authorizing the application.

This is typically only needed when the user is logging in to a third-party application rather than a first-party application. For example, when logging in to Gmail, you wouldn't expect Google to ask you whether it's okay for Gmail to know your account info, since both the application (Gmail) and the OAuth server are part of the same company's product. However if you are logging in to a third-party mailing list application that will send emails from your Gmail account, it becomes critical that you as the user are informed about what this third-party application will be granted access to and what it will be able to do with your account.

An authorization interface typically has the following components:

Website name and logo

The service should be easily recognizable by the user, since they need to know which service they are granting access to. However you identify your website on your main pages should be consistent with the authorization interface. Typically this is done by showing the application name and logo in a consistent location of the screen, and/or by using a consistent color scheme across the entire website.

User identification

If the user is already signed in, you should indicate this to the user. This may be something like showing their name and photo in the top corner of the screen, as you would in the rest of your website.

It is important that the user knows which account they are currently signed in as, in case they manage multiple accounts, so that they don't mistakenly authorize a different user account.

Application details

The authorization interface should clearly identify the application that is making the request. In addition to the developer-provided application name, it is usually a good idea to show the website and application's logo as well. This is information you will have collected when the developer registered the application. We discussed this in detail in Chapter 8, *Client Registration*.

One way to indicate more information about the application is to display the host name of the redirect URL. GitHub includes this in their authorization interface, saying "You will be redirected to example-app.com". This provides an additional hint to the user about whether this is really the app they are intending to use. Without this information, users are opened up to a sort of phishing attack where a malicious application can pretend to be a legitimate application by registering with the legit app's name and tricking users into authorizing the malicious app instead.

The requested scope

The scope values provided in the authorization request should be clearly displayed to the user. The scope values are typically short strings representing certain access, so a more human-readable version should be shown to the user.

For example, if a service defines a scope of "private" to mean read access to private profile data, then the authorization server should say something along the lines of "this application will be able to view your private profile data." If the scope explicitly allows write access, that should also be identified in the description, such as "this application will be able to edit your profile data."

If no scope is present, but your service still grants some basic level of access to a user's account, you should include a message describing what the app will get access to. If omitting scope means the only thing the app gets is user identification, you can include a message to the effect of "this application would like you to sign in" or "this application would like to know your basic profile information."

See Chapter 10, *Scope,* for more information on how to effectively use scope in your service.

The requested or effective lifetime

The authorization server has to make a decision about how long the authorization will be valid, how long the access tokens will last and how long refresh tokens will last.

Most services do not automatically expire authorizations, and instead expect the user to periodically review and revoke access to apps they no longer want to use. However some services provide limited authorization lifetime by default, and either allow the application to request a longer duration, or force users to re-authorize the app after the authorization is expired.

Whatever your decision about the lifetime of the authorization, you should make it clear to the user how long the app will be able to act on the user's behalf. This can be something as simple as a sentence that says "this application will be able to access your account until you revoke access," or "this application will be able to access your account for one week." See Access Token Lifetime on page 142 for more information about token lifetimes.

Allow / Deny

Lastly, the authorization server should provide two buttons to the user, to allow or deny the request.

If the user approves the request, the authorization server will create a temporary authorization code and redirect the user back to the application. If the user clicks "deny," the server will redirect back to the application with an error code in the URL. The next section, Authorization Response on page 99 goes into details of how this response should be handled.

The Authorization Response

Once the user has finished logging in and approving the request, the authorization server is ready to redirect the user back to the application.

Authorization Code Response

If the request is valid and the user grants the authorization request, the authorization server generates an authorization code and redirects the user back to the application, adding the authorization code and the application's "state" value to the redirect URL.

Generating the Authorization Code

The authorization code must expire shortly after it is issued. The OAuth 2.0 spec recommends a maximum lifetime of 10 minutes, but in practice, most services set the expiration much shorter, around 30-60 seconds. The authorization code itself can be of any length, but the length of the codes should be documented.

Because authorization codes are meant to be short-lived and single-use, you could implement them as self encoded tokens. With this technique, you can avoid storing authorization codes in a database, and instead, encode all of the necessary information into the authorization code itself. You can use either a built-in encryption library of your server-side environment, or a standard such as JSON Web Signature (JWS). However, since this authorization code is only meant to be used by the authorization server, it can often be simpler to implement them as short strings stored in a server-side cache that's accessible to the authorization endpoint and token endpoint.

In any case, the information that will need to be associated with the authorization code is the following.

- `client_id` - The client ID (or other client identifier) that requested this code
- `redirect_uri` - The redirect URL that was used. This needs

Chapter 9: Authorization

to be stored since the access token request must contain the same redirect URL for verification when issuing the access token. See Redirect URL Validation on page 125 for more information.
- **User info** - Some way to identify the user that this authorization code is for, such as a user ID.
- **Expiration Date** - The code needs to include an expiration date so that it only lasts a short time.
- **Unique ID** - The code needs its own unique ID of some sort in order to be able to check if the code has been used before. A database ID or a random string is sufficient.
- **PKCE: `code_challenge` and `code_challenge_method`** - When supporting PKCE, these two values provided by the application need to be stored so that they can be verified when issuing the access token later.

Once you've generated the authorization code, either by creating a JWS-encoded string, or by generating a random string and storing the associated information in a database, you'll need to redirect the user to the application's redirect URL specified. The parameters to be added to the query string of the redirect URL are as follows:

code

This parameter contains the authorization code which the client will later exchange for an access token.

state

If the initial request contained a state parameter, the response must also include the exact value from the request. The client will be using this to associate this response with the initial request.

For example, the authorization server redirects the user by sending the following HTTP response.

```
HTTP/1.1 302 Found
Location: https://example-app.com/redirect
?code=g0ZGZmNjVmOWI&state=dkZmYxMzE2
```

Implicit Grant Type Response

With the Implicit grant (`response_type=token`) the authorization server generates an access token immediately and redirects to the callback URL with the token and other access token attributes in the fragment.

For example, the authorization server redirects the user by sending the following HTTP response (extra line breaks for display purposes).

```
HTTP/1.1 302 Found
Location: https://example-app.com/redirect
  #access_token=MyMzFjNTk2NTk4ZTYyZGI3
  &state=dkZmYxMzE2
  &token_type=Bearer
  &expires_in=86400
```

You can see that this is much more dangerous than issuing a temporary one-time-use authorization code. Since there are many more ways an attacker can steal data out of an HTTP redirect compared to intercepting an HTTPS request, it's much riskier using this option compared to the authorization code flow.

From the authorization server's point of view, at the point it creates the access token and sends the HTTP redirect, it has no way of knowing whether or not the redirect was successful and the correct application has received the access token. It's kind of tossing the access token up into the air and crossing its fingers that the app catches it. This is in contrast to the authorization code method, where even though the authorization server can't guarantee the authorization code wasn't stolen, it can at least prevent a stolen authorization code from being useful by requiring a client secret or the PKCE code verifier. This provides a much greater level of security since the authorization server can now be more confident that it won't be giving access tokens away to attackers.

For these reasons as well as more documented in OAuth 2.0 for Browser-Based Apps *(https://datatracker.ietf.org/doc/html/draft-ietf-oauth-browser-based-apps)*, it is recommended that the Implicit flow no longer be used.

Error Response

There are two different kinds of errors to handle. The first kind of error is when the developer did something wrong when creating the authorization request. The other kind of error is when the user rejects the request (clicks the "Deny" button).

If there is something wrong with the syntax of the request, such as the `redirect_uri` or `client_id` is invalid, then it's important not to redirect the user and instead you should show the error message directly. This is to avoid letting your authorization server be used as an open redirector.

If the `redirect_uri` and `client_id` are both valid, but there is still some other problem, it's okay to redirect the user back to the redirect URI with the error in the query string.

When redirecting back to the application to indicate an error, the server adds the following parameters to the redirect URL:

error

a single ASCII error code from the following list:

- `invalid_request` - the request is missing a parameter, contains an invalid parameter, includes a parameter more than once, or is otherwise invalid.
- `access_denied` - the user or authorization server denied the request
- `unauthorized_client` - the client is not allowed to request an authorization code using this method, for example if a confidential client attempts to use the implicit grant type.
- `unsupported_response_type` - the server does not support obtaining an authorization code using this method, for example if the authorization server never implemented the implicit grant type.
- `invalid_scope` - the requested scope is invalid or unknown.
- `server_error` - instead of displaying a 500 Internal Server Error page to the user, the server can redirect with this error code.

- `temporarily_unavailable` - if the server is undergoing maintenance, or is otherwise unavailable, this error code can be returned instead of responding with a 503 Service Unavailable status code.

error_description

The authorization server can optionally include a human-readable description of the error. This parameter is intended for the developer to understand the error, and is not meant to be displayed to the end user. The valid characters for this parameter are the ASCII character set except for the double quote and backslash, specifically, hex codes 20-21, 23-5B and 5D-7E.

error_uri

The server can also return a URL to a human-readable web page with information about the error. This is intended for the developer to get more information about the error, and is not meant to be displayed to the end user.

state

If the request contained a state parameter, the error response must also include the exact value from the request. The client may use this to associate this response with the initial request.

Example

For example, if the user denied the authorization request, the server would construct the following URL and send an HTTP redirect response like the below (newlines in the URL are for illustration purposes).

```
HTTP/1.1 302 Found
Location: https://example-app.com/redirect?error=access_denied
  &error_description=The+user+denied+the+request
  &error_uri=https%3A%2F%2Fauthorization-server.com
  %2Ferror%2Faccess_denied
  &state=wxyz1234
```

Security Considerations

Below are some known issues that should be taken into consideration when building an authorization server.

In addition to the considerations listed here, there is more information available in the OAuth 2.0 Thread Model and Security Considerations *(https://datatracker.ietf.org/doc/html/rfc6819)* RFC as well as OAuth 2.0 Security Best Current Practice *(https://datatracker.ietf.org/doc/html/draft-ietf-oauth-security-topics)*.

Phishing Attacks

One potential attack against OAuth servers is a phishing attack. This is where an attacker makes a web page that looks identical to the service's authorization page, which typically contain username and password fields. Then, through various means, the attacker can trick the user in to visiting the page. Unless the user can inspect the address bar of the browser, the page may look otherwise identical to the genuine authorization page, and the user may enter their username and password.

One way attackers can attempt to trick the user into visiting the counterfeit server is by embedding this phishing page in an embedded web view in a native application. Since embedded web views don't show the address bar, the user then has no way to visually confirm they are on the legitimate site. This is unfortunately common in mobile applications, and often justified by the developer wanting to provide a better user experience by keeping the user in the application through the entire login process.

Some OAuth providers encourage third party applications to either open a web browser or launch the provider's native application instead of allowing them to embed an authorization page in a web view.

Countermeasures

Ensure the authorization server is served via https to avoid DNS spoofing.

The authorization server should educate developers of the risks of phishing attacks, and can take steps to prevent the page from being embedded in native applications or in iframes.

Users should be educated about the dangers of phishing attacks, and should be taught best practices such as only accessing applications that they trust, and periodically reviewing the list of applications they've authorized to revoke access to apps they no longer use. See Revoking Access on page 153 for more information.

The service may want to validate third-party applications prior to allowing other users to use the application. Services such as Instagram and Dropbox currently do this, where upon initial creation of an application, the app is only usable by the developer or other whitelisted user accounts. After the app is submitted for approval and reviewed, then it can be used by the whole user base of the service. This gives the service a chance to inspect how the application interacts with the service.

Clickjacking

In a clickjacking attack, the attacker creates a malicious website in which it loads the authorization server URL in a transparent iframe above the attacker's web page. The attacker's web page is stacked below the iframe, and has some innocuous-looking buttons or links, placed very carefully to be directly under the authorization server's confirmation button. When the user clicks the misleading visible button, they are actually clicking the invisible button on the authorization page, thereby granting access to the attacker's application. This allows the attacker to trick the user into granting access without their knowledge.

Countermeasures

This kind of attack can be prevented by ensuring the authorization URL is always loaded directly in a native browser, and not embedded in an iframe. Newer browsers have the ability for the authorization server to set an HTTP header, `X-Frame-Options`, and older browsers can use common JavaScript "frame-busting" techniques.

Redirect URL Manipulation

An attacker can construct an authorization URL using a client ID that belongs to a known good application, but set the redirect URL to a URL under the control of the attacker. If the authorization server does not validate redirect URLs, and the attacker uses the "token" response type, the user will be returned to the attacker's application with the access token in the URL. If the client is a public client, and the attacker intercepts the authorization code, then the attacker can also exchange the code for an access token.

Another similar attack is when the attacker can spoof the user's DNS, and the registered redirect is not an https URL. This would allow the attacker to pretend to be the valid redirect URL, and steal the access token that way.

The "Open Redirect" attack is when the authorization server does not require an exact match of the redirect URL, and instead allows an attacker to construct a URL that will redirect to the attacker's website. Whether or not this ends up being used to steal authorization codes or access tokens, this is also a danger in that it can be used to launch other unrelated attacks. More details about the Open Redirect attack can be found at *https://oauth.net/advisories/2014-1-covert-redirect/*.

Countermeasures

The authorization server must require that one or more redirect URLs are registered by the application, and only redirect to an exact match of a previously registered URL.

The authorization server should also require that all redirect URLs are https. Since this can sometimes be a burden during development, it is also acceptable to allow non-https redirect URLs while the application is "in development" and can only be accessed by the developer, and then require that the redirect URL is changed to an https URL before the application is published and available to other users.

Chapter 10
Scope

Scope is a way to limit an app's access to a user's data. Rather than granting complete access to a user's account, it is often useful to give apps a way to request a more limited scope of what they are allowed to do on behalf of a user.

Some apps only use OAuth in order to identify the user, so they only need access to a user ID and basic profile information. (See Chapter 22, *OpenID Connect*, for an example.) Other apps may need to know more sensitive information such as the user's birthday, or they may need the ability to post content on behalf of the user, or modify profile data. Users will be more willing to authorize an application if they know exactly what the application can and cannot do with their account. Scope is a way to control access and help the user identify the permissions they are granting to the application.

It's important to remember that scope is not the same as the internal permissions system of an API. Scope is a way to limit what an application can do within the context of what a user can do. For example, if you have a user in the "customer" group, and the application is requesting the "admin" scope, the OAuth server is not going to create an access token with the "admin" scope, because that user is not allowed to use that scope themselves.

Scope should be thought of as the application requesting permission from the user who's using the app.

Defining Scopes

Scope is a mechanism to let an application request limited access to a user's data.

The challenge when defining scopes for your service is to not get carried away with defining too many scopes. Users need to be able to understand what level of access they are granting to the application, and this will be presented to the user in some sort of list. When presented to the user, they need to actually understand what is going on and not get overwhelmed with information. If you over-complicate it for users, they will just click "ok" until the app works, and ignore any warnings.

Read vs. Write

Read vs write access is a good place to start when defining scopes for a service. Typically read access to a user's private profile information is treated with separate access control from apps wanting to update the profile information.

Apps that need to be able to create content on behalf of a user (for example, third-party Twitter apps that post tweets to a user's timeline) need a different level of access from apps that only need to read a user's public data.

Restricting Access to Sensitive Information

Often a service will have various aspects of a user account that have different levels of security. For example, GitHub (*https://developer.github.com/v3/oauth/#scopes*) has a separate scope that allows applications to have access to private repos. By default, applications don't have access to private repos unless they ask for that scope, so users can feel comfortable knowing that only apps they choose can access their private repos belonging to their organization.

GitHub provides a separate scope that allows applications to delete repos, so users can rest assured that random applications can't go around deleting their repos either.

Dropbox *(https://www.dropbox.com/developers/reference/oauth-guide)* provides a way for applications to restrict themselves to only be able to edit files in a single folder. This provides a way that users can try out apps that use Dropbox as a storage or syncing mechanism without worrying about the application potentially having the ability to read all their files.

Selectively Enabling Access by Functionality

A great use of scope is to selectively enable access to a user's account based on the functionality needed. For example, Google offers a set of scopes for their various services such as Google Drive, Gmail, YouTube, etc. This means applications that need to access the YouTube API won't necessarily also be able to access the user's Gmail account.

Google's API is a great example of effectively using scope. For a full list of the scopes that the Google OAuth API supports, visit their OAuth 2.0 Playground at *https://developers.google.com/oauthplayground/*

Limiting Access to Billable Resources

If your service provides an API that may cause the user to incur charges, scope is a great way to protect against applications abusing this.

Let's use an example of a service that provides advanced capabilities that use licensed content, in this case one that provides an API that aggregates demographic data for a given area. The user racks up charges as the service is used, and the cost is based on the size of the area being queried. A user signing in to an app that uses a completely different part of the API would want to ensure this app is not able to use the demographics API, since that would cause that user to incur charges. The service should in this case define a special scope, say, "demographics". The demographics API should only respond to API requests from tokens that contain this scope.

In this example, the demographics API could use the token introspection endpoint (described in Chapter 18, *Token Introspection Endpoint*) to look up the list of scopes that are valid for this token. If the response does not include "demographics" in the list of scopes, the endpoint would reject the request with an HTTP 403 response.

User Interface

The interface that the user sees when authorizing an app needs to clearly display the list of scopes that are being requested by the application. The user may not be aware of all of the possibilities of scopes that the service provides, so it's best to make this text as clear and straightforward as possible, avoiding jargon and abbreviations.

If the request grants the application full access to a user's account, or access to a substantial part of their account such as being able to do everything except change their password, the service should make it abundantly clear.

Figure 10-1: Dropbox Authorization Interface

For example, the first sentence on the Dropbox authorization UI (Figure 10-1) is "Example OAuth App would like access to the files and folders in your Dropbox" with a "Learn More" link that links to a help page describing exactly what access the application will have.

The Flickr authorization interface (Figure 10-2) shows three things the user is granting to the app when they sign in, and clearly shows permission the app will *not* have. The benefit of showing this is the user can be reassured the app they're authorizing won't be able to do potentially destructive operations.

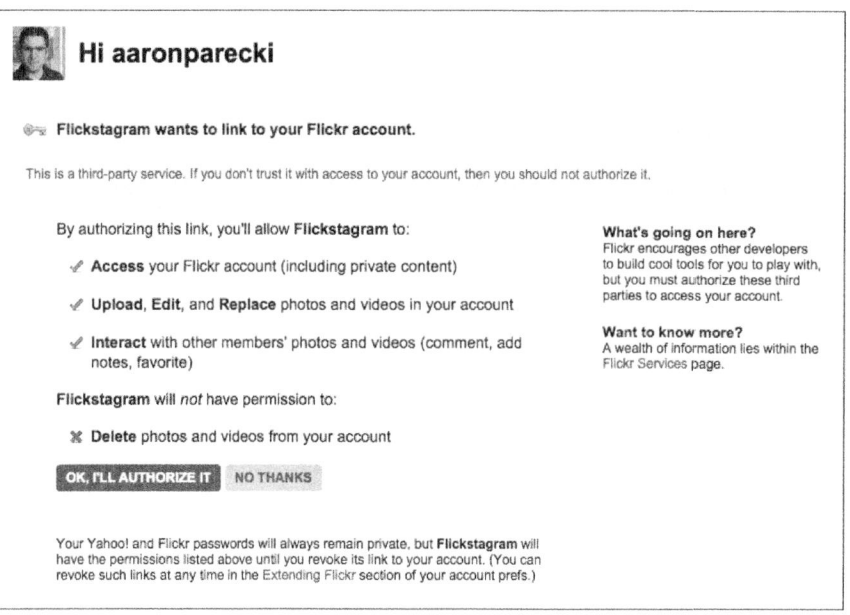

Figure 10-2: Flickr Authorization Interface

In Figure 10-3 we can see that GitHub has done a great job of providing detailed information about the scopes a user is granting. Each scope requested gets a section on the page with the name, an icon, a short description highlighting whether this is read-only or read-write, and a dropdown to see a more detailed explanation.

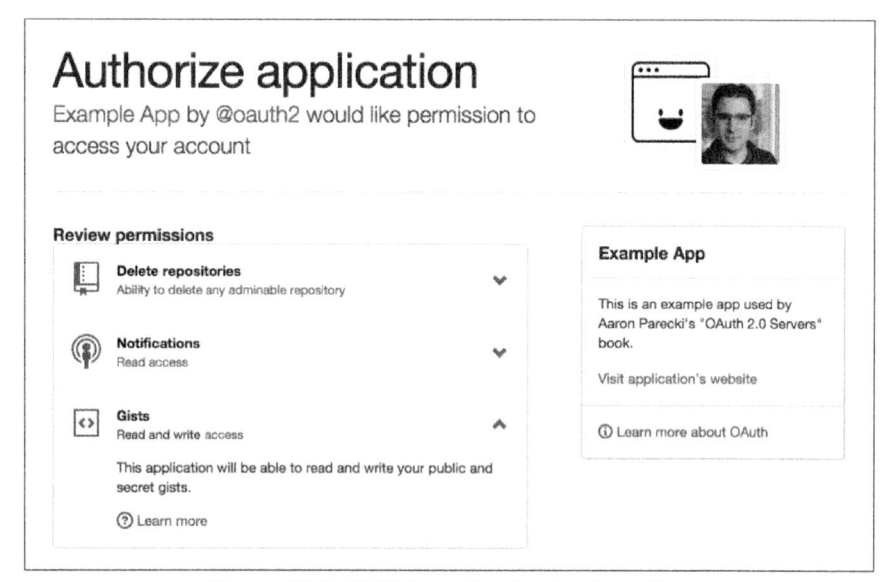

Figure 10-3: GitHub Authorization Interface

Google has a single authorization endpoint for all of their services including the Gmail API, Google Drive, Youtube, etc. Their authorization interface (Figure 10-4) displays each scope in a list, and includes an "information" icon you can click to get more information about the particular scope.

Figure 10-4: Google Authorization Interface

Clicking the information icon presents an overlay that describes in detail what this scope allows, shown in Figure 10-5.

You can see there are a number of ways you can provide the user with information about the scope of the OAuth grant, and various services have taken quite different approaches. Be sure to consider the privacy and security requirements of your application when deciding what level of detail you will include about the scope.

Figure 10-5: More information about the Google authorization request

Checkboxes

While seemingly an underused feature, the OAuth 2.0 spec explicitly allows the authorization server to grant an access token with less scope than the application requests. This leaves room for some interesting possibilities.

Before the development of the OAuth 2.0 spec began, OAuth 1 was deployed at Twitter, and the Twitter app ecosystem was growing quickly. When creating a Twitter app, you would choose whether your app needed read+write access or just read access to your users' accounts. This was a mechanism that led to the development of OAuth 2.0's concept of scope. However, this implementation was rather limiting, since apps would either request write access or not, and the user might simply reject the request if they did not want to grant the app write access.

There quickly developed a common anti-pattern of Twitter apps that only used the write access to post a tweet advertising the app. One of the more infamous occurrences of this was in 2010, when the app "Twifficiency," which claimed to "calculate your twitter efficiency based upon your twitter activity" spiraled out of control. You would sign in to the app with your Twitter account, and it would crawl through your past tweets and analyze them. However, it also automatically tweeted out "My Twifficiency score is __%. What's yours?" with a link to the website. Many people were not even aware the app was doing this, or that they had granted this app permission to post to their account. This caused the app to go viral, since the followers of anyone who used the app would see it in their timeline.

Many people were upset about this, and complained loudly on Twitter. Ben Ward, a developer at Yahoo at the time, went one step further, and created a mockup of a potential user interface (Figure 10-6) that could solve this problem, and wrote a brief blog post explaining it. *https://benward.uk/blog/tumblr-968515729*

In the post, Ward described a user interface that would allow the application to request specific permissions, and the user could choose to grant or not grant each one. This would allow users to sign in to an application but not grant the ability for it to post to their account at first. Later, if the user did want to allow the app to post, the app could provide a mechanism to re-authorize the user on Twitter. Ward was hired at Twitter a few months later.

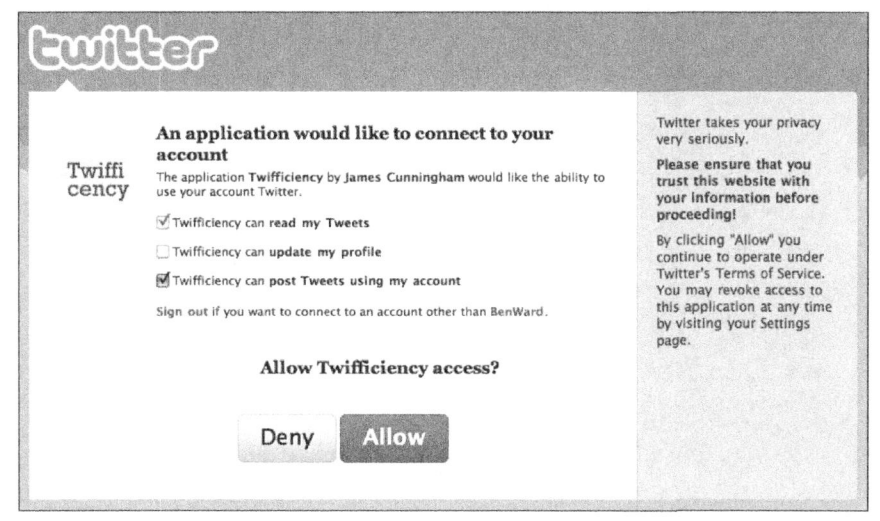

Figure 10-6: A a potential Twitter authorization interface that allows the user to customize the scopes granted to the application, by Ben Ward

This post stirred up some discussion among several people involved in the development of the OAuth specs, in a Google Buzz thread which now only exists on archive.org. *https://oauth.net/r/twitter-oauth-buzz*

To this day, Twitter still does not provide this kind of granular authorization. However, other services have begun to implement similar things, giving the user more control during the authorization flow rather than making it look like a "click OK to continue" dialog.

Facebook

Facebook supports a variation on this idea by providing a simple UI for the initial screen, but allows users to click to edit the scopes the application will be granted (Figure 10-7.)

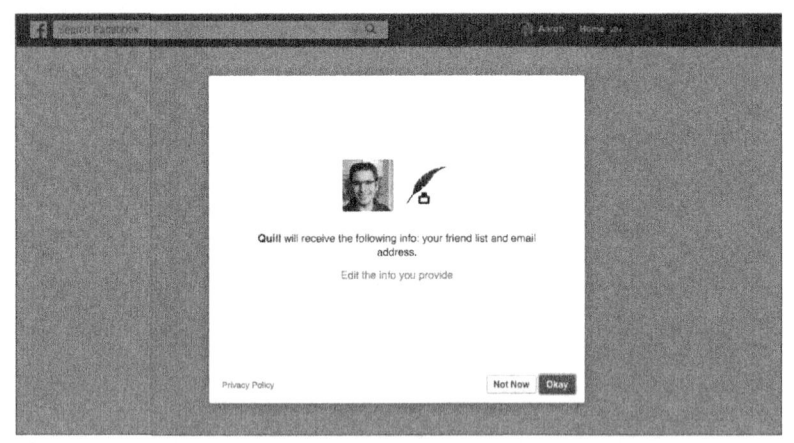

Figure 10-7: Facebook's initial authorization prompt

If you click "Edit the info you provide", you are taken to an interface (Figure 10-8) that lists each scope the application requested, and you can un-check them as desired. In the screenshot below, I've chosen to not allow the application to see my list of friends.

Figure 10-8: Clicking "Edit" allows the user to customize the scopes granted

Only the scopes the application requested appear in this list. This provides a better experience for users, since they are able to maintain control and better understand how applications can use their account.

FitBit

FitBit tracks many aspects of a user's health, such as step count, heart rate, food and drink consumed, sleep quality, weight, and more. The FitBit API provides access to all this data to third party applications. Because many third-party apps will be reading or writing only certain kinds of data, such as a wifi scale that only needs to write weight entries, FitBit provides granular scopes so that a user can grant access to only certain parts of their profile.

FitBit's authorization screen, shown in Figure 10-9 allows the user to selectively grant or deny access to each particular scope that the application is requesting.

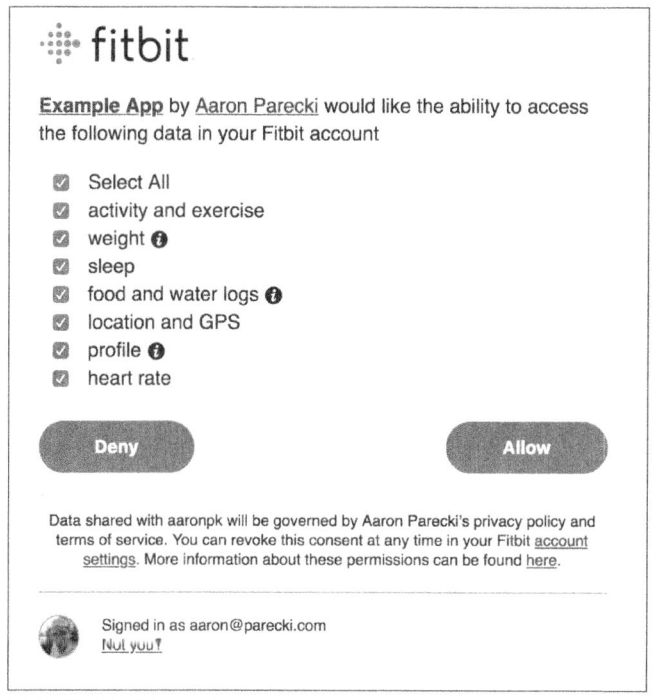

Figure 10-9: FitBit allows the user to un-check any scopes that they do not want to grant to the application

GitHub

GitHub has described in a blog post in 2013 that they have plans for allowing users to edit the scopes, however as of 2019, there has been no follow-up. *https://developer.github.com/changes/ 2013-10-04-oauth-changes-coming/*

Giving your users the ability to choose which scopes are granted is a great way to make people feel more comfortable with using third party apps. A checkbox next to each scope is sufficient, or you can move the controls to a separate screen like Facebook. You'll need to ensure that when you send the access token response to the client, it includes the list of scopes granted if it's different from what the application requested. See Access Token Response on page 133 for more details.

Chapter 11
Redirect URLs

Redirect URLs are a critical part of the OAuth flow. After a user successfully authorizes an application, the authorization server will redirect the user back to the application. Because the redirect URL will contain sensitive information, it is critical that the service doesn't redirect the user to arbitrary locations.

The best way to ensure the user will only be redirected to appropriate locations is to require the developer to register one or more redirect URLs when they create the application. In these sections we will cover how to handle redirect URLs for mobile applications, how to validate redirect URLs, and how to handle errors.

Registration

In order to avoid exposing users to open redirector attacks, you must require developers register one or more redirect URLs for the application. The authorization server must never redirect to any other location. Registering a New Application on page 79 describes creating a registration form to allow developers to register redirect URLs for their applications.

If an attacker can manipulate the redirect URL before the user reaches the authorization server, they could cause the server to redirect the user to a malicious server which would send the authorization code to the attacker. This is one way attackers can try to intercept an OAuth exchange and steal access tokens. If the authorization endpoint does not limit the URLs that it will redirect to, then it's considered an "open redirector", and can be used in combination with other things to launch attacks that aren't even related to OAuth necessarily.

Valid Redirect URLs

When you build the form to allow developers to register redirect URLs, you should do some basic validation of the URL that they enter.

Registered redirect URLs may contain query string parameters, but must not contain anything in the fragment. The registration server should reject the request if the developer tries to register a redirect URL that contains a fragment.

Note that for native and mobile apps, the platform may allow a developer to register a URL scheme such as `myapp://` which can then be used in the redirect URL. This means the authorization server should allow arbitrary URL schemes to be registered in order to support registering redirect URLs for native apps. See Chapter 15, *Mobile and Native Apps,* for more information.

Per-Request Customization

Often times a developer will think that they need to be able to use a different redirect URL on each authorization request, and will try to change the query string parameters per request. This is not the intended use of the redirect URL, and should not be allowed by the authorization server. The server should reject any authorization requests with redirect URLs that are not an exact match of a registered URL. See Redirect URL Validation on page 125 for more information.

If a client wishes to include request-specific data in the redirect URL, it can instead use the "state" parameter to store data that will be included after the user is redirected. It can either encode the data in the state parameter itself, or use the state parameter as a session ID to store the state on the server.

Redirect URLs for Native Apps

Native applications are clients installed on a device, such as a desktop application or mobile phone application. There are a few things to keep in mind when supporting native apps related to security and user experience.

The authorization endpoint normally redirects the user back to the client's registered redirect URL. Depending on the platform, native apps can either claim a URL pattern, or register a custom URL scheme that will launch the application. For example, an iOS application may register a custom protocol such as `myapp://` and then use a `redirect_uri` of `myapp://callback`.

App-Claimed https URL Redirection

Some platforms, (Android, and iOS as of iOS 9), allow the app to override specific URL patterns to launch the native application instead of a web browser. For example, an application could register `https://app.example.com/auth` and whenever the web browser attempts to redirect to that URL, the operating system launches the native app instead.

If the operating system does support claiming URLs, this method should be used. If the operating system does some level of validation that the developer had control over this web URL, then this allows the identity of the native application to be guaranteed by the operating system. If the operating system does not support this, then the app will have to use a custom URL scheme instead.

Custom URL Scheme

Most mobile and desktop operating systems allow apps to register a custom URL scheme that will launch the app when a URL with that scheme is visited from the system browser.

Using this method, the native app starts the OAuth flow as normal, by launching the system browser with the standard authorization code parameters. The only difference is that the redirect URL will be a URL with the app's custom scheme.

When the authorization server sends the `Location` header intending to redirect the user to `myapp://callback?code=....`, the phone will launch the application and the app will be able to resume the authorization process, parsing the access token from the URL and storing it internally.

Custom URL Scheme Namespaces

Since there is no centralized method of registering URL schemes, apps have to do their best to choose URL schemes that won't conflict with each other.

Your service can help by requiring the URL scheme to follow a certain pattern, and only allow the developer to register a custom scheme that matches that pattern.

For example, Facebook generates a URL scheme for every app based on the app's client ID. For example, `fb00000000://` where the numbers correspond to the app's client ID. This provides a reasonably sure method of generating globally unique URL schemes, since other apps are unlikely to use a URL scheme with this pattern.

Another option for apps is to use the reverse domain name pattern with a domain that is under the control of the app's publisher, resulting in a URL scheme of `com.example.myapp` for example. This is also something that can be enforced by the service if you wish.

Validation

There are three cases when you'll need to validate redirect URLs.

- When the developer registers the redirect URL as part of creating an application
- In the authorization request
- When the application exchanges an authorization code for an access token

Redirect URL Registration

As discussed in Creating an Application on page 79, the service should allow developers to register one or more redirect URLs when creating the application. The only restriction on the redirect URL is that it cannot contain a fragment component. The service must allow developers to register redirect URLs with custom URL schemes in order to support native applications on some platforms.

Authorization Request

When the application starts the OAuth flow, it will direct the user to your service's authorization endpoint. The request will have several parameters in the URL, including a redirect URL.

At this point, the authorization server must validate the redirect URL to ensure the URL in the request matches one of the registered URLs for the application. The request will also have a `client_id` parameter, so the service should look up the redirect URLs based on that. It is entirely possible for an attacker to craft an authorization request with one app's client ID and the attacker's redirect URL, which is why registration is required.

The service should look for an exact match of the URL, and avoid matching on only part of the specific URL. (The client can use the state parameter if it needs to customize each request.) Simple string matching is sufficient since the redirect URL can't be customized per request. All the server needs to do is check that the redirect URL in the request matches one of the redirect URLs the developer entered when registering their application.

If the redirect URL is not one of the registered redirect URLs, then the server must immediately show an error indicating such, and not redirect the user. This avoids having your authorization server be used as an open redirector *(https://oauth.net/advisories/2014-1-covert-redirect/)*.

Granting Access Tokens

The token endpoint will get a request to exchange an authorization code for an access token. This request will contain a redirect URL as well as the authorization code. As an added measure of security, the server should verify that the redirect URL in this request matches exactly the redirect URL that was included in the initial authorization request for this authorization code. If the redirect URL does not match, the server rejects the request with an error.

Chapter 12
Access Tokens

Access tokens are the thing that applications use to make API requests on behalf of a user. The access token represents the authorization of a specific application to access specific parts of a user's data.

Access tokens do not have to be of any particular format, although there are different considerations for different options which will be discussed later in this chapter. As far as the client application is concerned, the access token is an opaque string, and it will take whatever the string is and use it in an HTTP request. The resource server will need to understand what the access token means and how to validate it, but applications will never be concerned with understanding what an access token means.

Access tokens must be kept confidential in transit and in storage. The only parties that should ever see the access token are the application itself, the authorization server, and resource server. The application should ensure the storage of the access token is not accessible to other applications on the same device. The access token can only be used over an HTTPS connection, since passing it over a non-encrypted channel would make it trivial for third parties to intercept.

The token endpoint is where apps make a request to get an access token for a user. This section describes how to verify access token requests and how to return the appropriate response and errors.

Authorization Code Request

The authorization code grant is used when an application exchanges an authorization code for an access token. After the user returns to the application via the redirect URL, the application will get the authorization code from the URL and use it to request an access token. This request will be made to the token endpoint.

Request Parameters

The access token request will contain the following parameters.

grant_type (required)

The `grant_type` parameter must be set to "authorization_code".

code (required)

This parameter is the authorization code that the client previously received from the authorization server.

redirect_uri (possibly required)

If the redirect URL was included in the initial authorization request, the service must require it in the token request as well. The redirect URL in the token request must be an exact match of the redirect URL that was used when generating the authorization code. The service must reject the request otherwise.

code_verifier (required for PKCE support)

If the client included a `code_challenge` parameter in the initial authorization request, it must now prove it has the secret used to generate the hash by sending it in the POST request. This is the plaintext string that was used to calculate the hash that was previously sent in the `code_challenge` parameter.

`client_id` (required if no other client authentication is present)

If the client is authenticating via HTTP Basic Auth or some other method, then this parameter is not required. Otherwise, this parameter is required.

If the client was issued a client secret, then the server must authenticate the client. One way to authenticate the client is to accept another parameter in this request, `client_secret`. Alternately the authorization server can use HTTP Basic Auth. Technically the spec allows the authorization server to support any form of client authentication, and mentions public/private key pair as an option. In practice, most consumer servers support the simpler methods of authenticating clients using either or both of the methods mentioned here. For more advanced methods of authenticating the client, refer to RFC 7523 which defines a method of using a signed JWT as client authentication.

Verifying the authorization code grant

After checking for all required parameters, and authenticating the client if the client was issued credentials, the authorization server can continue verifying the other parts of the request.

The server then checks if the authorization code is valid and has not expired. The service must then verify that the authorization code provided in the request was issued to the client identified. Lastly, the service must ensure the redirect URL parameter present matches the redirect URL that was used to request the authorization code.

For PKCE support, the authorization server should calculate the SHA256 hash of the `code_verifier` presented in this token request, and compare that with the `code_challenge` presented in the authorization request. If they match, the authorization server can be confident that it's the same client making this token request that made the original authorization request.

If everything checks out, the service can generate an access token and respond.

Example

The following example shows an authorization grant request for a confidential client.

```
POST /oauth/token HTTP/1.1
Host: authorization-server.com

grant_type=authorization_code
&code=xxxxxxxxxxx
&redirect_uri=https://example-app.com/redirect
&code_verifier=Th7UHJdLswIYQxwSg29DbK1a_d9o41uNMTRmuH0PM8zyoMAQ
&client_id=xxxxxxxxxx
&client_secret=xxxxxxxxxx
```

See Access Token Response on page 133 for details on the parameters to return when generating an access token or responding to errors.

Security Considerations

Preventing replay attacks

If an authorization code is used more than once, the authorization server must deny the subsequent requests. This is easy to accomplish if the authorization codes are stored in a database or cached, since they can simply be marked as used or deleted.

If you are implementing self-encoded authorization codes, you'll need to keep track of whether an authorization code has already been used. One way to accomplish this by caching the authorization code for the lifetime of the code. This way when verifying authorization codes, we can first check if they have already been used by checking the cache for the code. Once the code reaches its expiration date, it will no longer be in the cache, but we can reject it based on the expiration date anyway.

If an authorization code is used more than once, it should be treated as an attack. If possible, the service should revoke the previous access tokens that were issued from this authorization code.

Password Grant

The Password grant is used when the application exchanges the user's username and password for an access token. This is exactly the thing OAuth was created to prevent in the first place, so you should never allow third-party apps to use this grant.

Supporting the Password grant is very limiting, as there is no way to add multifactor authorization to this flow, and your options for detecting brute force attacks are more limited. This flow should not be used in practice.

The latest *OAuth 2.0 Security Best Current Practice (https://oauth.net/2/oauth-best-practice/)* spec actually recommends against using the Password grant entirely, and it is being removed in the OAuth 2.1 update.

Request Parameters

The access token request will contain the following parameters.

- `grant_type` (required) - The `grant_type` parameter must be set to "password".
- `username` (required) - The user's username.
- `password` (required) - The user's password.
- `scope` (optional) - The scope requested by the application.
- Client Authentication (required if the client was issued a secret)

If the client was issued a secret, then the client must authenticate this request. Typically the service will allow either additional request parameters `client_id` and `client_secret`, or accept the client ID and secret in the HTTP Basic Auth header.

Example

The following is an example password grant the service would receive.

```
POST /oauth/token HTTP/1.1
    Host: authorization-server.com

    grant_type=password
    &username=user@example.com
    &password=1234luggage
    &client_id=xxxxxxxxxx
    &client_secret=xxxxxxxxxx
```

See Access Token Response on page 133 for details on the parameters to return when generating an access token or responding to errors.

Client Credentials

The Client Credentials grant is used when applications request an access token to access their own resources, not on behalf of a user.

Request Parameters

grant_type (required)

The `grant_type` parameter must be set to `client_credentials`.

scope (optional)

Your service can support different scopes for the client credentials grant. In practice, not many services actually support this.

Client Authentication (required)

The client needs to authenticate themselves for this request. Typically the service will allow either additional request parameters `client_id` and `client_secret`, or accept the client ID and secret in the HTTP Basic auth header.

Example

The following is an example authorization code grant the service would receive.

```
POST /oauth/token HTTP/1.1
Host: authorization-server.com

grant_type=client_credentials
&client_id=xxxxxxxxxx
&client_secret=xxxxxxxxxx
```

See Access Token Response on page 133 for details on the parameters to return when generating an access token or responding to errors.

Access Token Response

Successful Response

If the request for an access token is valid, the authorization server needs to generate an access token (and optional refresh token) and return these to the client, typically along with some additional properties about the authorization.

The response with an access token should contain the following properties:

- `access_token` (required) The access token string as issued by the authorization server.
- `token_type` (required) The type of token this is, typically just the string "Bearer".
- `expires_in` (recommended) If the access token expires, the server should reply with the number of seconds the access token is valid for.
- `refresh_token` (optional) If the access token will expire, then it is useful to return a refresh token which applications can use to obtain another access token.

- `scope` (optional) If the scope the user granted is identical to the scope the app requested, this parameter is optional. If the granted scope is different from the requested scope, then this parameter is required.

When responding with an access token, the server must also include the additional `Cache-Control: no-store` HTTP header to ensure clients do not cache this request.

For example, a successful token response may look like the following:

```
HTTP/1.1 200 OK
Content-Type: application/json
Cache-Control: no-store

{
  "access_token": "MTQ0NjJkZmQ5OTM2NDE1ZTZjNGZmZjI3",
  "token_type": "Bearer",
  "expires_in": 3600,
  "refresh_token": "IwOGYzYTlmM2YxOTQ5MGE3YmNmMDFkNTVk",
  "scope": "create"
}
```

Access Tokens

The format for OAuth 2.0 Bearer tokens is actually described in a separate spec, RFC 6750 *(https://datatracker.ietf.org/doc/html/rfc6750)*. There is no defined structure for the token required by the spec, so you can generate a string and implement tokens however you want. The valid characters in a bearer token are alphanumeric, and the following punctuation characters:

```
-._~+/
```

A simple implementation of Bearer Tokens is to generate a random string and store it in a database along with the associated user and scope information, or more advanced systems may use self-encoded tokens, described on page 137, where the token string itself contains all the necessary info.

Chapter 12: Access Tokens

Unsuccessful Response

If the access token request is invalid, such as the redirect URL didn't match the one used during authorization, then the server needs to return an error response.

Error responses are returned with an HTTP 400 status code (unless specified otherwise), with `error` and `error_description` parameters. The `error` parameter will always be one of the values listed below.

- `invalid_request` - The request is missing a parameter so the server can't proceed with the request. This may also be returned if the request includes an unsupported parameter or repeats a parameter.
- `invalid_client` - Client authentication failed, such as if the request contains an invalid client ID or secret. Send an HTTP 401 response in this case.
- `invalid_grant` - The authorization code (or user's password for the password grant type) is invalid or expired. This is also the error you would return if the redirect URL given in the authorization grant does not match the URL provided in this access token request.
- `invalid_scope` - For access token requests that include a scope (password or client_credentials grants), this error indicates an invalid scope value in the request.
- `unauthorized_client` - This client is not authorized to use the requested grant type. For example, if you restrict which applications can use the Implicit grant, you would return this error for the other apps.
- `unsupported_grant_type` - If a grant type is requested that the authorization server doesn't recognize, use this code. Note that unknown grant types also use this specific error code rather than using the `invalid_request` above.

There are two optional parameters when returning an error response, `error_description` and `error_uri`. These are meant to give developers more information about the error, not intended to be shown to end users. However, keep in mind that many developers will pass this error text straight on to end users no matter how much you warn them, so it is a good idea to make sure it is at least somewhat helpful to end users as well.

The `error_description` parameter can only include ASCII characters, and should be a sentence or two at most describing the circumstance of the error. The `error_uri` is a great place to link to your API documentation for information about how to correct the specific error that was encountered.

The entire error response is returned as a JSON string, similar to the successful response. Below is an example of an error response.

```
HTTP/1.1 400 Bad Request
Content-Type: application/json
Cache-Control: no-store

{
  "error": "invalid_request",
  "error_description": "Request was missing the
    'redirect_uri' parameter.",
  "error_uri": "See the full API docs at
    https://authorization-server.com/docs/access_token"
}
```

Self-Encoded Access Tokens

Self-encoded tokens provide a way to avoid storing tokens in a database by encoding all of the necessary information in the token string itself. The main benefit of this is that API servers are able to verify access tokens without doing a database lookup on every API request, making the API much more easily scalable.

The benefit of OAuth 2.0 Bearer Tokens is that applications don't need to be aware of how you've decided to implement access tokens in your service. This means it's possible to change your implementation later without affecting clients.

If you already have a distributed database system that is horizontally scalable, then you may not gain any benefits by using self-encoded tokens. In fact, using self-encoded tokens if you've already solved the distributed database problem will only introduce new issues, as invalidating self-encoded tokens becomes an additional hurdle.

There are many ways to self-encode tokens. The actual method you choose is only important to your implementation of your authorization server and resource server, since the token information is not exposed to external developers.

The most common way to implement self-encoded tokens is to use the JWS spec, creating a JSON-serialized representation of all the data you want to include in the token, and signing the resulting string with a private key known only to your authorization server.

RFC 9068 *(https://datatracker.ietf.org/doc/html/rfc9068)* defines a standard way to use JWTs as access tokens, based on the real-world deployment experience of a number of large OAuth providers. This spec defines a data structure to use when including claims about authentication, authorization, and identity. See *https://oauth.net/2/jwt-access-tokens/ (https://oauth.net/2/jwt-access-tokens/)* for further details.

JWT Access Token Encoding

The code below is written in PHP and uses the Firebase PHP-JWT *(https://github.com/firebase/php-jwt)* library to encode and verify tokens. You'll need to include that library in order to run the sample code.

In practice, the authorization server will have a private key it uses for signing tokens, and the resource server would fetch the public key from the authorization server metadata to use to validate the tokens. In this example we generate a new private key each time and validate tokens in the same script. In reality you'd need to store the private key somewhere to use the same key to sign tokens consistently.

```
<?php
use \Firebase\JWT\JWT;

# Generate a private key to sign the token.
# The public key would need to be published at the authorization
# server if a separate resource server needs to validate the JWT

$private_key = openssl_pkey_new([
  'digest_alg' => 'sha256',
  'private_key_bits' => 1024,
  'private_key_type' => OPENSSL_KEYTYPE_RSA
]);

# Set the user ID of the user this token is for
$user_id = 1000;

# Set the client ID of the app that is generating this token
$client_id = 'https://example-app.com';

# Provide the list of scopes this token is valid for
$scope = 'read write';

$token_data = array(

  # Issuer (the authorization server identifier)
  'iss' => 'https://' . $_SERVER['PHP_SELF'],

  # Expires At
  'exp' => time()+7200, // Valid for 2 hours
```

```php
    # Audience (The identifier of the resource server)
    'aud' => 'api://default',

    # Subject (The user ID)
    'sub' => $user_id,

    # Client ID
    'client_id' => $client_id,

    # Issued At
    'iat' => time(),

    # Identifier of this token
    'jti' => microtime(true).'.'.bin2hex(random_bytes(10)),

    # The list of OAuth scopes this token includes
    'scope' => $scope
);

$token_string = JWT::encode($token_data, $private_key, 'RS256');
```

This will result in a string such as:

```
eyJ0eXAiOiJKV1QiLCJhbGciOiJSUzI1NiJ9.eyJpc3MiOiJodH
RwczpcL1wvYXV0aG9yaXphdGlvbi1zZXJ2ZXIuY29tXC8iLCJle
HAiOjE2MzczNDQ1NzIsImF1ZCI6ImFwaTpcL1wvZGVmYXVsdCIs
InN1YiI6MTAwMCwiY2xpZW50X2lkIjoiaHR0cHM6XC9cL2V4YW1
wbGUtYXBwLmNvbSIsImlhdCI6MTYzNzMzNzM3MiwianRpIjoiMT
YzNzMzNzM3Mi4yMDUxLjYyMGY1YTNkYzBlYmFhMDk3MzEyIiwic
2NvcGUiOiJyZWFkIHdyaXRlIn0.SKDO_Gu96WeHkR_Tv0d8gFQN
1SEdpN8S_h0IJQyl_5syvpIRA5wno0VDFi34k5jbnaY5WHn6Y91
2IOmg6tMO91KlYOU1MNdVhHUoPoNUzYtl_nNab7Ywe29kxgrekm
-67ZInDI8RHbSkL7Z_N9eZz_J8c3EolcsoIf-Dd5n9y_Y
```

This token is made up of three components, separated by periods. The first part describes the signature method used. The second part contains the token data. The third part is the signature.

For example, this token's first component is this JSON object:

```
{
  "typ": "JWT",
  "alg": "RS256"
}
```

The second component contains the actual data the API endpoint needs in order to process the request, such as user identification and scope access.

```
{
  "iss": "https://authorization-server.com/",
  "exp": 1637344572,
  "aud": "api://default",
  "sub": 1000,
  "client_id": "https://example-app.com",
  "iat": 1637337372,
  "jti": "1637337372.2051.620f5a3dc0ebaa097312",
  "scope": "read write"
}
```

The two components are then base64-encoded, and the JWT library calculates the RS256 signature of the two strings, then joins all three parts with a period:

```
eyJ0eXAiOiJKV1QiLCJhbGciOiJSUzI1NiJ9.eyJpc3MiOiJodH
RwczpcL1wvYXV0aG9yaXphdGlvbi1zZXJ2ZXIuY29tXC8iLCJle
HAiOjE2MzczNDQ1NzIsImF1ZCI6ImFwaTpcL1wvZGVmYXVsdCIs
InN1YiI6MTAwMCwiY2xpZW50X2lkIjoiaHR0cHM6XC9cL2V4YW1
wbGUtYXBwLmNvbSIsImlhdCI6MTYzNzMzNzM3MiwianRpIjoiMT
YzNzMzNzM3Mi4yMDUxLjYyMGY1YTNkYzBlYmFhMDk3MzEyIiwic
2NvcGUiOiJyZWFkIHdyaXRlIn0.SKDO_Gu96WeHkR_Tv0d8gFQN
1SEdpN8S_h0IJQyl_5syvpIRA5wno0VDFi34k5jbnaY5WHn6Y91
2IOmg6tMO91KlYOU1MNdVhHUoPoNUzYtl_nNab7Ywe29kxgrekm
-67ZInDI8RHbSkL7Z_N9eZz_J8c3EolcsoIf-Dd5n9y_Y
```

Decoding

Verifying the access token can be done by using the same JWT library. The library will decode and verify the signature at the same time, and throws an exception if the signature was invalid, or if the expiration date of the token has already passed.

You'll need the public key corresponding to the private key that signed the token. Typically you can fetch this from the authorization server's metadata document, but in this example we will derive the public key from the private key generated earlier.

Note: Anyone can read the token information by base64-decoding the middle section of the token string. For this reason, it's important that you do not store private information or information you do not want a user or developer to see in the token. If you want to hide the token information, you can use the JSON Web Encryption *(https://datatracker.ietf.org/doc/html/rfc7516)* spec to encrypt the data in the token.

```
$public_key = openssl_pkey_get_details($private_key)['key'];

try {
  # Note: You must provide the list of supported algorithms
  # in order to prevent an attacker from bypassing the signature
  # verification
  $token = JWT::decode($token_string, $public_key, ['RS256']);
  $error = false;
} catch(\Firebase\JWT\ExpiredException $e) {
  $token = false;
  $error = 'expired';
  $error_description = 'The token has expired';
} catch(\Firebase\JWT\SignatureInvalidException $e) {
  $token = false;
  $error = 'invalid';
  $error_description = 'The token provided was malformed';
} catch(Exception $e) {
  $token = false;
  $error = 'unauthorized';
  $error_description = $e->getMessage();
}

if($error) {
  header('HTTP/1.1 401 Unauthorized');
  echo json_encode(array(
    'error'=>$error,
    'error_description'=>$error_description
  ));
  die();
} else {
  // Now $token has all the data that we encoded in it originally
  print_r($token);
}
```

At this point, the API has all the information it needs such as the user ID, scope, etc, available to it, and didn't have to do a database lookup. Next it can verify the scope is sufficient to perform the requested operation, and can then process the request.

Invalidating Access Tokens

Because the token can be verified without doing a database lookup, there is no way to invalidate a token until it expires. You'll need to take additional steps to invalidate tokens that are self-encoded, such as temporarily storing a list of revoked tokens, which is one use of the `jti` claim in the token. See Refreshing Access Tokens on page 145 for more information.

Access Token Lifetime

When your service issues access tokens, you'll need to make some decisions as to how long you want the tokens to last. Unfortunately there is no blanket solution for every service. There are various tradeoffs that come with the different options, so you should choose the option (or combination of options) that best suit your application's need.

Short-lived access tokens and long-lived refresh tokens

A common method of granting tokens is to use a combination of access tokens and refresh tokens for maximum security and flexibility. The OAuth 2.0 spec recommends this option, and several of the larger implementations have gone with this approach.

Typically services using this method will issue access tokens that last anywhere from several hours to a couple weeks. When the service issues the access token, it also generates a refresh token that never expires and returns that in the response as well.

When the access token expires, the application can use the refresh token to obtain a new access token (Refreshing Access Tokens). It can do this behind the scenes, and without the user's involvement, so that it's a seamless process to the user.

The main benefit of this approach is that the service can use self-encoded access tokens which can be verified without a database lookup. However, this means there is no way to expire those tokens directly, so instead, the tokens are issued with a short expiration time so that the application is forced to continually refresh them, giving the service a chance to revoke an application's access if needed.

From the third-party developer's perspective, it is often frustrating to have to deal with refresh tokens. Developers tend to prefer the easy option of using access tokens that don't expire. In order to help mitigate these concerns, services will often build the token refreshing logic into their SDK, so that the process is transparent to developers.

In summary, use short-lived access tokens and long-lived refresh tokens when:

- you want to use self-encoded access tokens
- you want to limit the risk of leaked access tokens
- you will be providing SDKs that can handle the refresh logic transparently to developers

Short-lived access tokens and no refresh tokens

If you want to ensure users are aware of applications that are accessing their account, or require that the user re-authenticate at some regular interval, the service can issue relatively short-lived access tokens without refresh tokens. The access tokens may last anywhere from the current application session to a couple weeks. When the access token expires, the application will be forced to make the user sign in again, so that you as the service know the user is continually involved in re-authorizing the application.

Typically this option is used by services where there is a high risk of damage if a third-party application were to accidentally or maliciously leak access tokens. By requiring that users are constantly re-authorizing the application, the service can ensure that potential damage is limited if an attacker were to steal access tokens from the service.

By not issuing refresh tokens, this makes it impossible to applications to use the access token on an ongoing basis without the user in front of the screen. Applications that need access in order to continually sync data will be unable to do so under this method.

From the user's perspective, this is the option most likely to frustrate people, since it will look like the user has to continually re-authorize the application.

In summary, use short-lived access tokens with no refresh tokens when:

- you want to the most protection against the risk of leaked access tokens
- you want to force users to be aware of third-party access they are granting
- you don't want third-party apps to have offline access to users' data

Non-expiring access tokens

Non-expiring access tokens are the easiest method for developers, but the least secure. If you choose this option, it is important to consider the trade-offs you are making.

Even if the you intend on issuing access tokens that never expire for normal use, you'll still need to provide a mechanism to expire them under exceptional circumstances, such as if the user explicitly wants to revoke an application's access, or if a user account is deleted.

Non-expiring access tokens are much easier for developers testing their own applications. You can even pre-generate one or more non-expiring access tokens for developers and show it to them on the application details screen. This way they can immediately start making API requests with the token, and not worry about setting up an OAuth flow in order to start testing your API.

In summary, use non-expiring access tokens when:

- you have a mechanism to revoke access tokens arbitrarily
- you don't have a huge risk if tokens are leaked
- you want to provide an easy authentication mechanism to your developers
- you want third-party applications to have offline access to users' data

Refreshing Access Tokens

This section describes how to allow your developers to use refresh tokens to obtain new access tokens. If your service issues refresh tokens along with the access token, then you'll need to implement the Refresh grant type described here.

Request Parameters

The access token request will contain the following parameters.

grant_type (required)

The `grant_type` parameter must be set to "refresh_token".

refresh_token (required)

The refresh token previously issued to the client.

scope (optional)

The requested scope must not include additional scopes that were not issued in the original access token. Typically this will not be included in the request, and if omitted, the service should issue an access token with the same scope as was previously issued.

Client Authentication (required if the client was issued a secret)

Typically, refresh tokens are only used with confidential clients. However, since it is possible to use the authorization code flow without a client secret, the refresh grant may also be used by clients that don't have a secret. If the client was issued a secret, then the client must authenticate this request. Typically the service will allow either additional request parameters `client_id` and `client_secret`, or accept the client ID and secret in the HTTP Basic auth header. If the client does not have a secret, then no client authentication will be present in this request.

Verifying the refresh token grant

After checking for all required parameters, and authenticating the client if the client was issued a secret, the authorization server can continue verifying the other parts of the request.

The server then checks whether the refresh token is valid, and has not expired. If the refresh token was issued to a confidential client, the service must ensure the refresh token in the request was issued to the authenticated client.

If everything checks out, the service can generate an access token and respond. The server may issue a new refresh token in the response, but if the response does not include a new refresh token, the client assumes the existing refresh token will still be valid.

Example

The following is an example refresh grant the service would receive.

```
POST /oauth/token HTTP/1.1
Host: authorization-server.com

grant_type=refresh_token
&refresh_token=xxxxxxxxxxx
&client_id=xxxxxxxxxx
&client_secret=xxxxxxxxxx
```

Response

The response to the refresh token grant is the same as when issuing an access token (page 133). You can optionally issue a new refresh token in the response, or if you don't include a new refresh token, the client assumes the current refresh token will continue to be valid.

Chapter 13
Listing Authorizations

Once users have begun to authorize multiple applications giving many apps various kinds of access to their account, it becomes necessary to provide a way to allow the user to manage the apps that have access. This is usually presented to the user in an account settings page or an account privacy page.

You won't find anything in the OAuth 2.0 spec that requires users be able to revoke accesss or even suggests how to do this, so instead we'll look at several major API providers for inspiration on how to accomplish this.

Most providers have a page which lists all applications the user has authorized to their account. Usually there is some information displayed about the application, and information meant to give context to the user about when and why this application has access.

Google

Google provides a list of applications you've authorized on your account at *https://myaccount.google.com/permissions*, as shown in Figure 13-1.

The list shows the application icon, name, and a summary of the scope that the application is granted. Clicking on one of them expands that section to show more details.

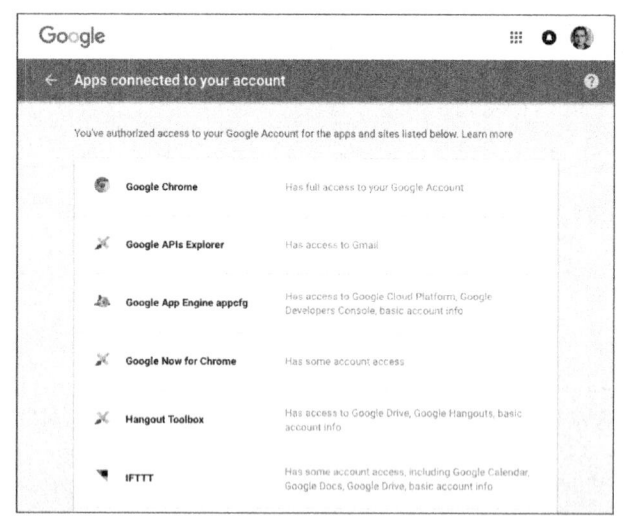

Figure 13-1: A sample list of applications you've authorized to access your Google account

Figure 13-2: Details of one application's access to your Google account

Figure 13-2 shows a more detailed list of scopes that have been granted, as well as the date that you authorized the application.

Twitter

Twitter provides a list of applications you've authorized at *https://twitter.com/settings/applications*.

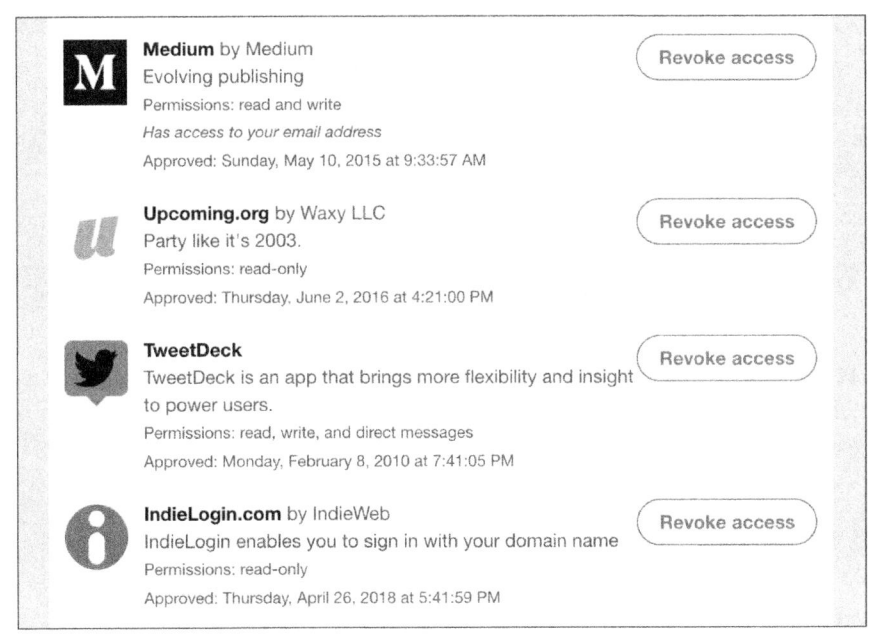

Figure 13-3: A sample list of applications you've authorized to access your Twitter account

Twitter shows the scope that was granted (read-only, read/write, read/write/direct messasges), as well as whether the app can see your email address. The list includes the date you authorized the application. This makes it easy for users to revoke credentials from apps they haven't used in a while.

GitHub

GitHub provides a list of applications you've authorized at *https://github.com/settings/applications*.

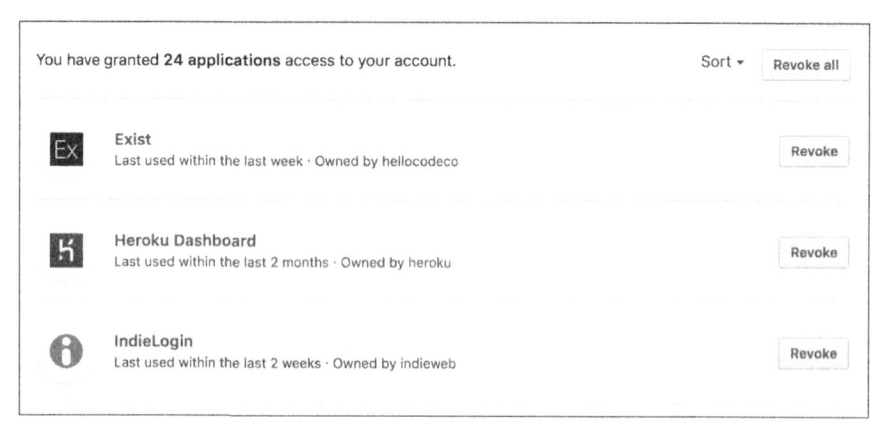

Figure 13-4: A sample list of applications you've authorized to access your GitHub account

The list that GitHub provides, shown in Figure 13-4, includes a description of the last time the application was used, to give you an idea of whether you can safely revoke an application's credentials if it hasn't been used in a while.

Clicking on an application provides more details about that application's access.

In Figure 13-5 you can see the permissions (scope) the application has for your account.

You can find links to other services' authorization pages at *https://indieweb.org/appaccess*.

All of these services provide a way for the user to revoke a particular application's access to their account. The next section covers revoking access in more detail.

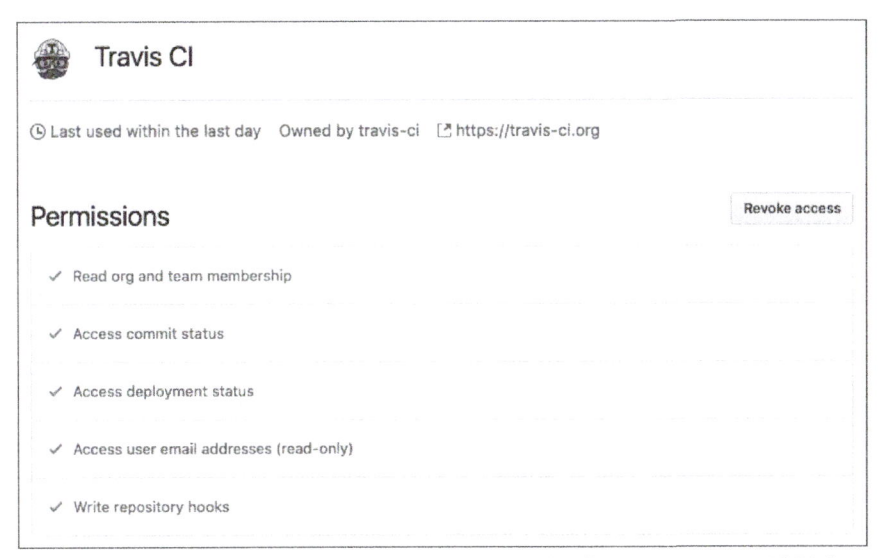

```
┌─────────────────────────────────────────────────────────────────┐
│  🌀  Travis CI                                                  │
│                                                                 │
│  ⏱ Last used within the last day   Owned by travis-ci   ↗ https://travis-ci.org  │
│                                                                 │
│  Permissions                                     [Revoke access]│
│                                                                 │
│    ✓ Read org and team membership                               │
│                                                                 │
│    ✓ Access commit status                                       │
│                                                                 │
│    ✓ Access deployment status                                   │
│                                                                 │
│    ✓ Access user email addresses (read-only)                    │
│                                                                 │
│    ✓ Write repository hooks                                     │
│                                                                 │
└─────────────────────────────────────────────────────────────────┘
```

Figure 13-5: Details of one application authorized to access your GitHub account

Revoking Access

There are a few reasons you might need to revoke an application's access to a user's account.

- The user explicitly wishes to revoke the application's access, such as if they've found an application they no longer want to use listed on their authorizations page
- The developer wants to revoke all user tokens for their application
- The developer deleted their application (page 87)
- You as the service provider have determined an application is compromised or malicious, and want to disable it

Depending on how you've implemented generating access tokens, revoking them will work in different ways.

Token Database

If you store access tokens in a database, then it is relatively easy to revoke all tokens that belong to a particular user. You can write a query that finds and deletes tokens belonging to the user, such as looking in the token table for their `user_id`. Assuming your resource server validates access tokens by looking them up in the database, then the next time the revoked client makes a request, their token will fail to validate.

Self-Encoded Tokens

If the authorization server issues self-encoded tokens, then revoking access to a particular application is a little harder.

If you have a truly stateless mechanism of verifying tokens, and your resource server is validating tokens without sharing information with another system, then the only option is to wait for all outstanding tokens to expire, and prevent the application from being able to generate new tokens for that user by blocking any refresh token requests from that client ID. This is the primary reason to use extremely short-lived tokens when you are using self-encoded tokens.

If you can afford some level of statefulness, you could push a revocation list of token identifiers to your resource servers, and your resource servers can check that list when validating a token. The access token can contain a unique ID (e.g. the `jti` claim) which can be used to keep track of individual tokens. If you want to revoke a particular token, you would need to put that token's `jti` into a list somewhere that can be checked by your resource servers. Of course this means your resource servers are no longer doing a purely stateless check, so this may not be an option available for every situation.

You will also need to invalidate the application's refresh tokens that were issued along with an access token. Revoking the refresh token means the next time the application attempts to refresh the access token, the request for a new access token will be denied.

Chapter 14
The Resource Server

The resource server is the OAuth 2.0 term for your API server. The resource server handles authenticated requests after the application has obtained an access token.

Large scale deployments may have more than one resource server. Google's services, for example, have dozens of resource servers, such as Gmail, Google Calendar, Google Cloud platform, Google Maps, Google Drive, YouTube, and many others. Each of these resource servers are distinctly separate, but they all share the same authorization server.

Google Cloud APIs
Compute Engine API
BigQuery API
Cloud Storage Service
Cloud Datastore API
Cloud Deployment Manager API
Cloud DNS API
≈ More

Mobile APIs
Google Cloud Messaging
Google Play Game Services
Google Play Developer API
Google Places API for Android

Advertising APIs
AdSense Management API
DCM/DFA Reporting And Trafficking API
Ad Exchange Seller API
Ad Exchange Buyer API
DoubleClick Search API
DoubleClick Bid Manager API

Google Maps APIs
Google Maps Android API
Google Maps SDK for iOS
Google Maps JavaScript API
Google Places API for Android
Google Places API for iOS
Google Maps Roads API
≈ More

Social APIs
Google+ API
Blogger API
Google+ Pages API
Google+ Domains API

Other popular APIs
Analytics API
Translate API
Custom Search API
URL Shortener API
PageSpeed Insights API
Fusion Tables API
Web Fonts Developer API

Google Apps APIs
Drive API
Calendar API
Gmail API
Sheets API
Google Apps Marketplace SDK
Admin SDK
≈ More

YouTube APIs
YouTube Data API
YouTube Analytics API
YouTube Reporting API

Figure 14-1: Some of Google's APIs

Smaller deployments typically have only one resource server, and it's often built as part of the same code base or same deployment as the authorization server.

Verifying Access Tokens

The resource server will be getting requests from applications with an HTTP `Authorization` header containing an access token. The resource server needs to be able to verify the access token to determine whether to process the request, and find the associated user account, etc.

If you're using self-encoded access tokens (page 137), then verifying the tokens can be done entirely in the resource server without interacting with a database or external servers.

If your tokens are stored in a database, then verifying the token is simply a database lookup on the token table.

Another option is to use the Token Introspection spec described on page 181 to build an API to verify access tokens. This is a good way to handle verifying access tokens across a large number of resource servers, since it means you can encapsulate all of the logic of access tokens at your authorization server, exposing the information via an API to other parts of the system. The token introspection endpoint is intended to be used only internally, so you will want to protect it with some internal authorization, or only enable it on a server within the firewall of the system.

Verifying Scope

The resource server needs to know the list of scopes that are associated with the access token. The server is responsible for denying the request if the scopes in the access token do not include the required scope to perform the designated action.

The OAuth 2.0 spec does not define any scopes itself, nor is there a central registry of scopes. The list of scopes is up to the service to decide for itself. See Chapter 10, *Scope,* for more information.

Expired Tokens

If your service uses short-lived access tokens with long-lived refresh tokens, then you'll need to make sure to return the proper error response when an application makes a request with an expired token.

Return an HTTP 401 response with a `WWW-Authenticate` header as described below. If your API typically returns JSON responses, then you can also return a JSON body with the same error information.

```
HTTP/1.1 401 Unauthorized
WWW-Authenticate: Bearer error="invalid_token"
                  error_description="The access token expired"
Content-type: application/json

{
  "error": "invalid_token",
  "error_description": "The access token expired"
}
```

This will indicate to clients that their existing access token expired and that they should try to get a new one using their refresh token.

Error Codes and Unauthorized Access

If the access token does not allow access to the requested resource, or if there is no access token in the request, then the server must reply with an HTTP 401 response and include a `WWW-Authenticate` header in the response.

The minimum `WWW-Authenticate` header includes the string `Bearer`, indicating that a bearer token is required. The header can also indicate additional information such as a "realm" and "scope". The "realm" value is used in the traditional HTTP Authentication sense *(https://datatracker.ietf.org/doc/html/rfc7235)*. The "scope" value allows the resource server to indicate the list of scopes required to access the resource, so the application can request the appropriate scope from the user when starting the authorization flow. The response should also include an appropriate "error" value depending on the type of error that occurred.

- `invalid_request` (HTTP 400) - The request is missing a parameter, or is otherwise malformed.
- `invalid_token` (HTTP 401) - The access token is expired, revoked, malformed, or invalid for other reasons. The client can obtain a new access token and try again.
- `insufficient_scope` (HTTP 403) - The request requires additional scope that this access token was not issued.

For example:

```
HTTP/1.1 401 Unauthorized
WWW-Authenticate: Bearer realm="example",
                  scope="delete",
                  error="insufficient_scope"
```

If the request does not have authentication, then no error code or other error information is necessary.

```
HTTP/1.1 401 Unauthorized
WWW-Authenticate: Bearer realm="example"
```

Chapter 15
OAuth for Native Apps

This chapter describes some special considerations to keep in mind when supporting OAuth for native apps. Like browser-based apps, native apps can't use a client secret, as that would require that the developer ship the secret in their binary distribution of the application. It has been proven to be relatively easy to decompile and extract the secret. As such, native apps must use an OAuth flow that does not require a preregistered client secret.

The current industry best practice is to use the Authorization Flow along with the PKCE extension, omitting the client secret from the request, and to use an external user agent to complete the flow. An external user agent is typically the device's native browser, (with a separate security domain from the native app) so that the app cannot access the cookie storage or inspect or modify the page content inside the browser. Since the app can't reach inside the browser being used in this case, this provides the opportunity for the device to keep users signed in while authorizing different applications, so that they don't have to enter their credentials each time they authorize a new application.

In recent years, both iOS and Android have been working to further improve the user experience of OAuth for native apps by providing a native user agent that can be launched from within the application, while still being isolated from the application launching it. The result is that the user no longer needs to leave the application in order to launch a native browser that shares the system cookies. This was first added as `SFSafariViewController` in iOS 9, and later evolved to `SFAuthenticationSession` in iOS 11, and `ASWebAuthenticationSession` in iOS 12.

These recommendations for native apps are published as an RFC 8252 *(https://datatracker.ietf.org/doc/html/rfc8252)*, where these concepts are described in more explicit detail.

Use a System Browser

It used to be common practice for native apps to embed the OAuth interface in a web view inside the app. This approach has multiple problems, including that the client app can potentially eavesdrop on the user entering their credentials when signing in, or even present a false authorization page. Mobile operating system security is typically implemented in a way where the embedded web view doesn't share cookies with the system's native browser, so users have a worse experience because they need to enter their credentials each time as well.

The more secure and trusted way to accomplish the authorization flow is by launching a system browser. However, up until the addition of the specialized device APIs, this had the drawback of the user being popped out of the app and launching their browser, then redirecting back to the app, which is also not an ideal user experience.

Thankfully, the mobile platforms have been addressing the issue. There are now APIs available on iOS and Android for apps to launch a system browser but stay within the context of the application. The API does not not allow the client app to peek inside the browser, getting the security benefits of using an external browser and the user experience benefits of staying within the application the whole time.

Native app developers are strongly encouraged to use these special-purpose APIs, but if they can't for some reason, fall back to launching an external browser instead of an embedded web view.

Authorization servers should enforce this behavior by attempting to detect whether the authorization URL was launched inside an embedded web view and reject the request if so. The particular techniques for detecting whether the page is being visited in an embedded web view vs the system browser will depend on the platform, but usually involve inspecting the user agent header.

Redirect URLs

In order to support a wide range of types of native apps, your server will need to support registering three types of redirect URLs, each to support a slightly different use case.

HTTPS URL Matching

Both iOS and Android allow apps to register URL patterns that indicate the app should be launched whenver a system browser visits a URL that matches the registered pattern. This is commonly used by apps to "deep link" into the native app, such as the Yelp app opening to the restaurant's page when a Yelp URL is viewed in the browser.

This technique can also be used by apps to register URL a pattern that will launch the app when an authorization server redirects back to the app. If a platform provides this feature, this is the recommended choice for native apps, as this provides the most integrity that the app belongs to the URL it's matching. This also provides a reasonable fallback in the case that the platform doesn't support app-claimed URLs.

Custom URL Scheme

Some platforms allow apps to register a custom URL scheme which will launch the app whenever a URL with that scheme is opened in a browser or another app. Supporting redirect URLs with a custom URL scheme allows clients to launch an external browser to complete the authorization flow, and then be redirected back to the application after the authorization is complete. However this method is less secure than the HTTPS URL matching method, as there is no global registry of custom URL schemes to avoid conflicts between developers.

App developers should choose a URL scheme that is likely to be globally unique, and one which they can assert control over. Since operating systems typically do not have a registry of whether a particular app has claimed a URL scheme, it is theoretically possible for two apps to independently choose the same scheme, such as `myapp://`. If you want to help prevent collisions by app developers using custom schemes, you should recommend (or even enforce) that they use a scheme that is the reverse domain name pattern of a domain they control. At the very least, you can require that the redirect URL contains at least one . so as not to conflict with other system schemes such as `mailto` or `ftp`.

For example, if an app has a corresponding website called `photoprintr.example.org`, the reverse domain name that can be used as their URL scheme would be `org.example.photoprintr`. The redirect URL that the developer would register would then begin with `org.example.photoprintr://`. By enforcing this, you can help encourage developers to choose explicit URL schemes that won't conflict with other installed applications.

Apps that use a custom URL scheme will start the authorization request as normal, described in Authorization Request on page 89, but will provide a redirect URL that has their custom URL scheme. The authorization server should still verify that this URL was previously registered as an allowed redirect URL, and can treat it like any other redirect URL registered by web apps.

When the authorization server redirects the native app to the URL with the custom scheme, the operating system will launch the app and make the whole redirect URL accessible to the original app. The app can extract the authorization code just like a regular OAuth 2.0 client would.

Loopback URLs

Another technique native applications may use for supporting seamless redirects is opening a new HTTP server on a random port of the loopback interface. This is typically only done on desktop operating systems or for command line applications, as mobile operating systems typically do not provide this functionality to app developers.

This approach works well for command line apps as well as desktop GUI apps. The app will start an HTTP server and then begin the authorization request, setting the redirect URL to a loopback address such as `http://127.0.0.1:49152/redirect` and launching a browser. When the authorization server redirects the browser back to the loopback address, the application can grab the authorization code from the request.

In order to suppor this use case, the authorization server will have to support registering redirect URLs beginning with `http://127.0.0.1:[port]/` and `http://[::1]:[port]/`, and `http://localhost:[port]/`. The authorization server should allow an arbitrary path component as well as arbitrary port numbers. Note that in this case it is acceptable to use the HTTP scheme rather than HTTPS, as the request never leaves the device.

Registration

As with server-side apps, native apps must also register their redirect URL(s) with the authorization server. This means the authorization server will need to allow registered redirect URLs that match all the patterns described above, in addition to traditional HTTPS URLs for server-side apps.

When the authorization request is initiated at the authorization server, the server will validate all the request parameters, including the redirect URL given. The authorization should reject unrecognized URLs in the request, to help avoid an authorization code interception attack.

PKCE Extension

Since redirect URLs on native platforms have limited ability to be enforced, there is another technique for gaining additional security called Proof Key for Code Exchange, or PKCE for short, pronounced "pixie".

This technique involves the native app creating an initial random secret, and using that secret again when exchanging the authorization code for an access token. This way, if another app intercepts the authorization code, it will be unusable without the original secret.

Note that PKCE doesn't prevent app impersonation, it only prevents authorization codes from being used by a different app than the one that started the flow.

See Chapter 17, *Proof Key for Code Exchange*, for details.

Server Support Checklist

To summarize this chapter, your authorization server should support the following in order to fully support secure authorization for native apps.

- Allow clients to register custom URL schemes for their redirect URLs.
- Support loopback IP redirect URLs with arbitrary port numbers in order to support desktop apps.
- Don't assume native apps can keep a secret. Require all apps to declare whether they are public or confidential, and only issue client secrets to confidential apps.
- Support the PKCE extension, and require that public clients use it.
- Attempt to detect when the authorization interface is embedded in a native app's web view, instead of launched in a system browser, and reject those requests.

Chapter 16

OAuth for Browserless and Input-Constrained Devices

The OAuth 2.0 "Device Flow" extension enables OAuth on devices that have an Internet connection but don't have a browser or an easy way to enter text. If you've ever signed in to your YouTube account on a device such as an Apple TV, you've encountered this workflow already. Google was involved in the development of this extension, and has been an early implementer of it in production as well.

This flow is also seen on devices such as smart TVs, media consoles, picture frames, printers, or hardware video encoders. In this flow, the device instructs the user to open a URL on a secondary device such as a smartphone or computer in order to complete the authorization. There is no communication channel required between the user's two devices.

User Flow

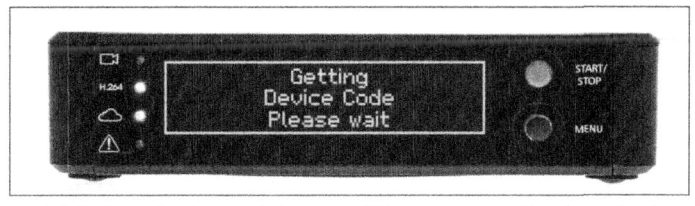

Figure 16-1: The device making an API request to obtain a device code

When you begin signing in on the device, such as this hardware video encoder, the device talks to the authorization server to get a device code, shown in Figure 16-1.

In Figure 16-2, we see that the device then shows you the code, along with a URL.

Figure 16-2: The device displays the device code and URL

Visiting that URL after you've signed in to your account shows an interface (Figure 16-3) that prompts you to enter the code that's displayed on the device.

Figure 16-3: Google prompts the user to enter the code

Once you enter the code and click "Next", you then see the standard OAuth authorization prompt that describes what scopes the application is requesting, as seen in Figure 16-4.

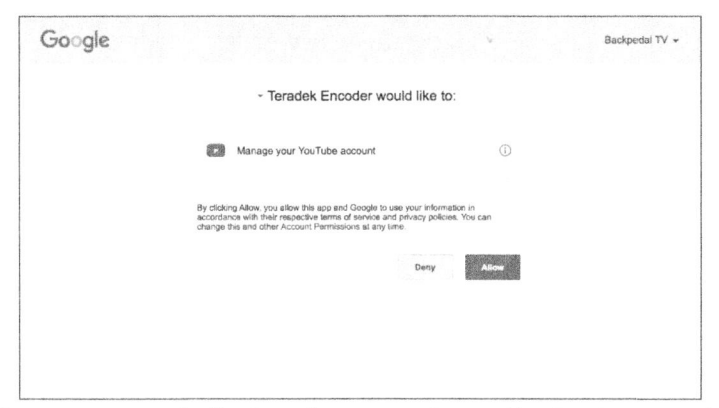

Figure 16-4: Google displays the scopes the application is requesting

Once you allow the request, the authorization server shows a message that says to return to your device, shown in Figure 16-5. A few seconds later, the device finishes up and you're signed in.

Figure 16-5: Google instructs the user to return to the device

Overall this is a pretty painless experience. Since you get to use whatever device you want to open the URL, you can use your primary computer or phone where you're likely already signed in to the authorization server. This also works with no data entry required on the device! No typing passwords or codes on what is likely a cumbersome tiny keyboard at best.

Let's walk through what's required by the device to make this work.

Authorization Request

First, the device makes a request to the authorization server to request the device code, identifying itself with its client ID, and requesting one or more scopes if it needs to.

```
POST /token HTTP/1.1
Host: authorization-server.com
Content-type: application/x-www-form-urlencoded

client_id=a17c21ed&
scope=create
```

The authorization server responds with a JSON payload containing the device code, the code the user will enter, the URL the user should visit, and a polling interval.

```
HTTP/1.1 200 OK
Content-Type: application/json
Cache-Control: no-store

{
  "device_code": "NGU5OWFiNjQ5YmQwNGY3YTdmZTEyNzQ3YzQ1YSA",
  "user_code": "BDWD-HQPK",
  "verification_uri": "https://authorization-server.com/device",
  "interval": 5,
  "expires_in": 1800
}
```

The device shows the `verification_uri` and `user_code` to the user on its display, directing the user to enter the code at that URL.

Token Request

While the device is waiting for the user to complete the authorization flow on their own computer or phone, the device meanwhile begins polling the token endpoint to request an access token.

The device makes a POST request with the `device_code` at the rate specified by `interval`. The device should continue requesting an access token until a response other than `authorization_pending` is returned, either the user grants or denies the request or the device code expires.

```
POST /token HTTP/1.1
Host: authorization-server.com
Content-type: application/x-www-form-urlencoded

grant_type=urn:ietf:params:oauth:grant-type:device_code&
client_id=a17c21ed&
device_code=NGU5OWFiNjQ5YmQwNGY3YTdmZTEyNzQ3YzQ1YSA
```

The authorization server will reply with either an error or an access token. The Device Flow spec defines two additional error codes beyond what is defined in OAuth 2.0 core, `authorization_pending` and `slow_down`.

If the device is polling too frequently, the authorization server will return the `slow_down` error.

```
HTTP/1.1 400 Bad Request
Content-Type: application/json
Cache-Control: no-store

{
  "error": "slow_down"
}
```

If the user has not either allowed or denied the request yet, the authorization server will return the `authorization_pending` error.

```
HTTP/1.1 400 Bad Request
Content-Type: application/json
```

```
Cache-Control: no-store

{
  "error": "authorization_pending"
}
```

If the user denies the request, the authorization server will return the `access_denied` error.

```
HTTP/1.1 400 Bad Request
Content-Type: application/json
Cache-Control: no-store

{
  "error": "access_denied"
}
```

If the device code has expired, the authorization server will return the `expired_token` error. The device can immediately make a request for a new device code.

```
HTTP/1.1 400 Bad Request
Content-Type: application/json
Cache-Control: no-store

{
  "error": "expired_token"
}
```

Finally, if the user allows the request, then the authorization server issues an access token like normal and returns the standard access token response.

```
HTTP/1.1 200 OK
Content-Type: application/json
Cache-Control: no-store

{
  "access_token": "AYjcyMzY3ZDhiNmJkNTY",
  "refresh_token": "RjY2NjM5NzA2OWJjuE7c",
  "token_type": "Bearer",
  "expires_in": 3600,
  "scope": "create"
}
```

Authorization Server Requirements

Supporting the Device Flow is not a huge amount of additional work for an authorization server. Here are a few things to keep in mind as you're adding support for the Device Flow to an existing authorization server.

Device Code Request

The device will make a request to the authorization server to obtain the set of verification codes needed for the flow. The following parameters are part of the request.

- `client_id` - Required, the client identifier as described in Chapter 8, *Client Registration*.
- `scope` - Optional, the scope of the request as described in Chapter 10, *Scope*.

After validating the client ID and scopes, the authorization server returns the response with the verification URL, device code and user code. There are a few optional parameters that the authorization server can return in addition to the example given above.

- `device_code` - Required, the verification code generated by the authorization server.
- `user_code` - Required, the code the user will enter on the device screen, should be relatively short. Typically 6-8 numbers and letters are used.
- `verification_uri` - Required, the URL on the authorization server that the user should visit to begin authorization. The user is expected to hand-enter this URL on their computer or mobile phone, so this should be a relatively short URL such as `example.com/device`.
- `expires_in` - Optional, the lifetime in seconds of the device code and user code.
- `interval` - Optional, the minimum amount of time in seconds that the client should wait between polling

requests to the token endpoint.

User Code

In many situations, the user's nearest device will be their mobile phone. Typically these interfaces are more limited than a full computer keyboard, like how the iPhone requires an additional tap to change the key case or switch to numeric entry. To help reduce data entry errors, and to speed up entry of the code, the character set of the user code should take into account these limitations, such as using only capital letters.

A reasonable character set to use for the device code is case insensitive A-Z characters, without vowels so as to avoid accidentally spelling words. This results in the base-20 character set BCDFGHJKLMNPQRSTVWXZ. When comparing the entered code, it is best to ignore any characters such as punctuation that are not in the character set. An example code following this guideline with an entropy of 20^8 is BDWD-HQPK. The authorization server should compare the entered string case-insensitively ignoring punctuation, so should allow the following as a match: bdwdhqpk.

Verification URL

The verification URL that the device will display should be as short as possible, and easy to remember. It will be displayed on potentially very small screens, and users will have to type it in manually on their computer or phone.

Note that the server should return a full URL including the URL scheme, although some devices may choose to trim that when displaying the URL. As such, the server should be configured to redirect http to https, and to serve on both the plain domain and with a www prefix in case the user mis-enters or the device omits that part of the URL.

Google's authorization server is a great example of a short URL that is easy to enter. The response from the code request is `https://www.google.com/device` but all the device needs to display is `google.com/device` and Google will redirect appropriately.

Optimization for Non-Textual Interfaces

Clients without a display, or with a non-textual display, obviously have no way to show a URL to the user. As such, there are some additional methods that could be used to communicate the verification URL and user code to the user.

The device may be able to broadcast the verification URL via NFC, or Bluetooth, or by displaying a QR code. In these cases, the device may include the user code as part of the verification URL using the parameter `user_code`. For example:

```
https://authorization-server.com/device?user_code=BDWD-HQPK
```

This way, when the user launches the URL, the user code can be pre-filled in the verification interface. It is recommended that the authorization server still require the user confirm the code rather than proceed automatically.

If the device has the ability to display the code, even if it cannot display a URL, then additional security is gained by prompting the user to confirm that the code on the verification interface matches the code displayed on their device. If that is not an option, then the authorization server can at least ask the user to confirm that they just requested to authorize a device.

Security Considerations

User Code Brute Forcing

Since the user code is hand-entered by the user into an interface that does not yet know about the device being authorized, precautions should be taken to avoid the possibility of a brute force attack against the user code.

Typically the user code will be a short code in order to be easily entered by hand. Short strings are more easily brute-forceable than long strings, so you should choose an appropriate rate limit based on the entopy of your API's user codes.

For example, with 8 characters out of the 20-character set described above, that provides approximately 34 bits of entropy. $\log_2(20^8) = 34.57$ You can use this formula to calculate the bits of entropy when choosing an acceptable rate limit.

Remote Phishing

It is possible for the device flow to be initiated on a device in the attacker's possession, in order to trick the user into authorizing the attacker's device. For example, the attacker might send an SMS instructing the user to visit a URL and enter the user code.

To mitigate this risk, it is recommended that the authorization interface make it very clear to the user that they are authorizing a physical device to access their account, in addition to the standard information included in the authorization interface described in User Interface on page 112.

Chapter 17
Protecting Apps with PKCE

Proof Key for Code Exchange (abbreviated PKCE, pronounced "pixie") is an extension to the authorization code flow to prevent CSRF and authorization code injection attacks. The technique involves the client first creating a secret on each authorization request, and then using that secret again when exchanging the authorization code for an access token. This way if the code is intercepted, it will not be useful since the token request relies on the initial secret.

PKCE was originally designed to protect the authorization code flow in mobile apps, and was later recommended to be used by single-page apps as well. In later years, it was recognized that its ability to prevent authorization code injection makes it useful for every type of OAuth client, even apps running on a web server that use a client secret. Because of its history in the use of mobile apps and single-page apps, it is sometimes incorrectly thought that PKCE is an alternative to a client secret. However PKCE is not a replacement for a client secret, and PKCE is recommended even if a client is using a client secret, since apps with a client secret are still susceptible to authorization code injection attacks.

The full spec is available as RFC 7636 (*https://datatracker.ietf.org/doc/html/rfc7636*). We'll cover a summary of the protocol below.

Authorization Request

When the application begins the authorization request, the client first creates a random string known as a "*code verifier*". This is a cryptographically random string using the characters `A-Z`, `a-z`, `0-9`, and the punctuation characters `-._~` (hyphen, period, underscore, and tilde), between 43 and 128 characters long.

Once the app has generated the code verifier, it uses that to derive the *code challenge*. For devices that can perform a SHA256 hash, the code challenge is a Base64-URL-encoded string of the SHA256 hash of the code verifier. Clients that do not have the ability to perform a SHA256 hash are permitted to use the plain code verifier string as the challenge, although that provides less security benefits so should really only be used if absolutely necessary.

Base64-URL-encoding is a minor variation on the typical Base64 encoding method. It starts with the same Base64-encoding method available in most programming languages, but uses URL-safe characters instead. You can implement a Base64-URL-encoding method by taking a Base64-encoded string and making the following modifications to the string: Take the Base64-encoded string, and change + to -, and / to _, then trim the trailing = from the end.

PHP

```
function base64_urlencode($str) {
  return rtrim(strtr(base64_encode($hash), '+/', '-_'), '=');
}
```

JavaScript

```
function base64_urlencode(str) {
  return btoa(String.fromCharCode.apply(null,
    new Uint8Array(str)))
      .replace(/\+/g, '-')
      .replace(/\//g, '_')
      .replace(/=+$/, '');
}
```

Now that the client has a *code challenge* string, it includes that and a parameter that indicates which method was used to generate the challenge (`plain` or `S256`) along with the standard parameters of the authorization request. This means a complete authorization request will include the following parameters.

- `response_type=code` - indicates that your server expects to receive an authorization code
- `client_id=` - The client ID you received when you first created the application
- `redirect_uri=` - Indicates the URL to return the user to after authorization is complete, such as `org.example.app://redirect`
- `state=` - A random string generated by your application, which you'll verify later
- `code_challenge=XXXXXXXXX` - The code challenge generated as previously described
- `code_challenge_method=S256` - either `plain` or `S256`, depending on whether the challenge is the plain verifier string or the SHA256 hash of the string.

The authorization server should recognize the `code_challenge` parameter in the request, and associate that with the authorization code it generates. When building an authorization server, you can either store this in the database along with the authorization code, or if you're using self-encoded authorization codes then it can be included in the code itself, although it must be encrypted in that case. (See The Authorization Response on page 99 for details.) The server returns the authorization code as normal, and does not include the challenge in the data returned.

Error Response

The authorization server can require that public clients must use the PKCE extension. This is really the only way to allow native apps to have a secure authorization flow without using the client secret, especially without the redirect URI security that's available with web-based clients. Since the authorization server should know that a specific client ID corresponds to a public client, it can deny authorization requests for public clients that do not contain a code challenge.

If the authorization server requires public clients to use PKCE, and the authorization request is missing the code challenge, then the server should return the error response with `error=invalid_request` and the `error_description` or `error_uri` should explain the nature of the error.

Authorization Code Exchange

The application will then exchange the authorization code for an access token. In addition to the parameters defined in Authorization Code Request (page 128), the client will also send the `code_verifier` parameter. A complete access token request will include the following parameters:

- grant_type=authorization_code - Indicates the grant type of this token request
- code - The client will send the authorization code it obtained in the redirect
- redirect_uri - The redirect URL that was used in the initial authorization request
- client_id - The application's registered client ID
- client_secret (optional) - The application's registered client secret if it was issued a secret
- code_verifier - The code verifier for the PKCE request which the app originally generated before the authorization request.

Since the `code_challenge` and `code_challenge_method` were associated with the authorization code initially, the server should already know which method to use to verify the `code_verifier`.

If the method is `plain`, then the authorization server needs only to check that the provided `code_verifier` matches the expected `code_challenge` string. If the method is S256, then the authorization server should take the provided `code_verifier` and transform it using the same hash method, then comparing it to the stored `code_challenge` string.

If the verifier matches the expected value, then the server can continue on as normal, issuing an access token and responding appropriately. If there is a problem, then the server responds with an `invalid_grant` error.

The PKCE extension does not add any new responses, so clients can always use the PKCE extension even if an authorization server does not support it.

Chapter 18
Token Introspection Endpoint

When an OAuth 2.0 client makes a request to the resource server, the resource server needs some way to verify the access token. The OAuth 2.0 core spec doesn't define a specific method of how the resource server should verify access tokens, it just mentions that it requires coordination between the resource and authorization servers. In some cases, especially with small services, both endpoints are part of the same system, and can share token information internally such as in a database. In larger systems where the two endpoints are on different servers, this has led to proprietary and non-standard protocols for communicating between the two servers.

The OAuth 2.0 Token Introspection extension *(https://datatracker.ietf.org/doc/html/rfc7662)* defines a protocol that returns information about an access token, intended to be used by resource servers or other internal servers.

An alternative to token introspection is to use a structured token format that is recognized by both the authorization server and resource server. The JWT Profile for OAuth 2.0 Access Tokens *(https://datatracker.ietf.org/doc/html/rfc9068)* is a recent RFC that describes a standardized format for access tokens using JWTs. This enables a resource server to validate access tokens without a network call, by validating the signature and parsing the claims within the structured token itself.

Introspection Endpoint

The token introspection endpoint needs to be able to return information about a token, so you will most likely build it in the same place that the token endpoint lives. The two endpoints need to either share a database, or if you have implemented self-encoded tokens, they will need to share the secret.

Token Information Request

The request will be a POST request containing just a parameter named "token". It is expected that this endpoint is not made publicly available to developers. Applications should not be allowed to use this endpoint since the response may contain privileged information that developers should not have access to. One way to protect the endpoint is to put it on an internal server that is not accessible from the outside world, or it could be protected with HTTP basic auth.

```
POST /token_info HTTP/1.1
Host: authorization-server.com
Authorization: Basic Y4NmE4MzFhZGFkNzU2YWRhN

token=c1MGYwNDJiYmYxNDFkZjVkOGI0MSAgLQ
```

Token Information Response

The Token Introspection Endpoint should respond with a JSON object with the properties listed below. Only the "active" property is required, the rest are optional. Some of the properties in the Introspection spec are specifically for JWT tokens, so we will only cover the basic ones here. You can also add additional properties in the response if you have additional information about a token that may be useful.

active

Required. This is a boolean value of whether or not the presented token is currently active. The value should be "true" if the token has been issued by this authorization server, has not been revoked by the user, and has not expired.

scope

A JSON string containing a space-separated list of scopes associated with this token.

client_id

The client identifier for the OAuth 2.0 client that the token was issued to.

username

A human-readable identifier for the user who authorized this token.

exp

The unix timestamp (integer timestamp, number of seconds since January 1, 1970 UTC) indicating when this token will expire.

Example Response

Below is an example of the response that the introspection endpoint would return.

```
HTTP/1.1 200 OK
Content-Type: application/json

{
  "active": true,
  "scope": "read write email",
  "client_id": "J8NFmU4tJVgDxKaJFmXTWvaHO",
  "username": "aaronpk",
```

```
  "exp": 1437275311
}
```

Error Response

If the introspection endpoint is publicly accessible, the endpoint must first validate the authentication in the request. If the authentication is invalid, the endpoint should respond with an HTTP 401 status code and an `invalid_client` response.

```
HTTP/1.1 401 Unauthorized
Content-Type: application/json

{
  "error": "invalid_client",
  "error_description": "Client authentication was invalid"
}
```

Any other error is considered an "inactive" token.

- The token requested does not exist or is invalid
- The token expired
- The token was issued to a different client than is making this request

In any of these cases, it is not considered an error response, and the endpoint returns simply an inactive flag with an HTTP 200 status.

```
HTTP/1.1 200 OK
Content-Type: application/json

{
  "active": false
}
```

Security Considerations

Using a token introspection endpoint means that any resource server will be relying on the endpoint to determine whether an access token is currently active or not. This means the introspection endpoint is solely responsible for deciding whether API requests will succeed. As such, the endpoint must perform all applicable checks against a token's state, such as checking whether the token has expired, verifying signatures, etc.

Token Fishing

If the introspection endpoint is left open and un-throttled, it presents a means for an attacker to poll the endpoint fishing for a valid token. To prevent this, the server must either require authentication of the clients using the endpoint, or only make the endpoint available to internal servers through other means such as a firewall.

Note that the resources servers are also a potential target of a fishing attack, and should take countermeasures such as rate limiting to prevent this.

Caching

Consumers of the introspection endpoint may wish to cache the response of the endpoint for performance reasons. As such, it is important to consider the performance and security trade-offs when deciding to cache the values. For example, shorter cache expiration times will result in higher security since the resource servers will have to query the introspection endpoint more frequently, but will result in an increased load on the endpoint. Longer expiration times leave a window open where a token may actually be expired or revoked, but still be able to be used at a resource server for the remaining duration of the cache time.

One way to mitigate this problem is for consumers to never cache the value beyond the expiration time of the token, which would have been returned in the "exp" parameter of the introspection response.

Limiting Information

The introspection endpoint does not necessarily need to return the same information for all queries of the same token. For example, two different resource servers (if they authenticate themselves when making the introspection request) may get different views of the state of the token. This can be used to limit the information about the token that is returned to a particular resource server. This makes it possible to have tokens that can be used at multiple resource servers without other servers ever knowing it is possible to be used at any other server.

Chapter 19
Creating Documentation

As you may have noticed after reading through this far, there are many places in the OAuth 2.0 spec where decisions are left up to the implementation. Many of these things were left under-specified in order to allow different implementations to make different decisions based on their own security requirements. The end result is that many OAuth 2.0 implementations are not actually interoperable, although in practice, many of the implementations have made the same decisions anyway, and are very similar.

Since there are many ways in which implementations can differ, as well as some parts of the process such as registering applications that have to happen manually, building good documentation for your service is essential.

This section covers the things you will need to document in order for a developer to be able to use your API. Some of these items can be documented inline in the appropriate interface (such as the interface developers use for client registration), and some are more appropriate to document in an "overview" section of your API docs.

Client Registration

How do developers register a new client application to obtain a client ID and optionally a secret?

- On a web page? Provide a link to the registration page.
- Programmatically? Your service may implement the

Dynamic Client Registration *(https://datatracker.ietf.org/doc/html/rfc7591)* spec, or have a proprietary API for registering applications
- Do you provide other mechanisms for developers to register applications? You will need to describe other ways to register apps if so.

Your service should at a minimum ask developers whether their application is a confidential or public client, and provide a way to register redirect URIs. Aside from those, you should document other information you collect about an application, and indicate which pieces of information are shown to the end-user during the authorization request.

- Application name
- Web page about the application
- Description
- Logo or other images
- Web page about the application's terms of use
- Other information?

Endpoints

There are two primary endpoints developers will be using during the OAuth process. Your **authorization endpoint** (page 89) is where the users will be directed to begin the authorization flow. After the application obtains an authorization code, it will exchange that code for an access token at the **token endpoint** (page 128). The token endpoint is also responsible for issuing access tokens for other grant types.

You need to let developers know the URLs for these two endpoints they will be using.

Client Authentication

When client authentication is required in a request, such as in the Authorization Code grant (page 128), there are two ways your service can accept the client ID and secret in the request. Your service can accept the authentication in an HTTP Basic Auth header using the client ID as the username and secret as the password, or by accepting the strings in the post body as `client_id` and `client_secret`. It is up to your service whether you want to accept either or both of these methods, so you need to tell your developers how you expect them to include this authentication in requests.

Additionally, your service may support other forms of client authentication, such as a public/private key pair. This is relatively uncommon in most consumer-grade OAuth 2.0 implementations, but the spec leaves that open as a possibility.

There are no requirements on the maximum or minimum length of client IDs and secrets issued to applications, so it's usually a good idea to let your developers know how big to expect these strings to be, so that they can store them appropriately.

Sizes of Strings

Since developers likely won't see an authorization code or access token until they've started writing code, you should document the maximum sizes of strings they will be encountering so they can plan accordingly.

- Client ID
- Client Secret
- Authorization Code
- Access Token

Response Types

Which response types does your service support? Typically services will support just the "code" response type for web-based and native apps, but you should make sure to point out whether your service requires PKCE for public clients.

Redirect URL Restrictions

Your service may place restrictions on registered redirect URLs that developers can use. For example, it is common that a service will disallow developers to use non-TLS http endpoints, or restrict those to be used by non-production applications. While supporting custom schemes is important for supporting native apps, some services disallow these as well. You should document any requirements you place on registering redirect URLs.

Default Scopes

If the developer does not specify a scope during the authorization request, the service may assume a default scope for that request. If that is the case, you should document what the default scope is.

The authorization server may ignore the scope that the developer requests, or add additional scopes beyond what is requested. The server may also allow the user to change the scope from what is requested. If any of these are possible, the service should clearly point that out to developers so that they can account for the access token possibly having different scopes than they had requested.

The service should also document the lifetime of the authorization codes issued, so developers know approximately how long they can expect the codes to last between being issued and being used. The authorization server may also prevent a code from being used more than once, and should document this if so.

Access Token Response

When you issue an access token, the access token response lists a number of parameters that are optional. You should document which of these your service supports, so developers know what to expect.

When does the response include an `expires_in` parameter? Your service may always include it if the token expires, or your service can document a default expiration developers should expect if this value is not in the response.

Does the response always include the scope of the access token that is granted? It's usually a good idea to return this in the response, but many services leave it out if the granted scope matches the requested scope. Either way, you should document the way your server behaves for this parameter.

Refresh Tokens

One of the more confusing or frustrating aspects for developers of OAuth 2.0 APIs is around refresh tokens. It's important to make it very clear how your service deals with refresh tokens if at all.

If your access tokens expire, you likely want to support refresh tokens so developers can build applications that continue to have access to users' accounts without the user continually re-authorizing the application.

You should clearly document which of the supported grant types include a refresh token in the response, and under what circumstances.

When your service issues a new access token in response to a refresh token grant, it is possible for your service to issue a new refresh token simultaneously, and expire the previous one. This means refresh tokens rotate out frequently, which may be desirable for your application. If this is the case, ensure developers know this will happen so they don't mistakenly assume the first refresh token they obtain will continue to work indefinitely.

Extension Grants

In addition to the four basic grant types, Authorization Code, Password, Client Credentials and Implicit, your service may support additional grant types.

Some grant types are standardized as extensions to OAuth 2.0, such as the Device Flow (page 165) and SAML *(https://datatracker.ietf.org/doc/html/draft-campbell-oauth-saml)*. Some services also implement their own custom grant types, such as when migrating a legacy API to OAuth 2.0. It's important to document the additional grant types your service supports, and provide documentation for how to use them.

Part III
Reference

Chapter 20

Terminology Reference

Roles

OAuth defines four roles:

- Resource owner (the user)
- Resource server (the API)
- Authorization server (issues access tokens and manages user logins)
- Client (the application)

The User

The OAuth 2.0 spec refers to the user as the "resource owner." The resource owner is the person who is giving access to some portion of their account. The resources in this case can be data (photos, documents, contacts), services (posting a blog entry, transferring funds), or any other resource requiring access restrictions. Any system that wants to act on behalf of the user must first get permission from them.

The API

The spec refers to what you typically think of as the main API as the "resource server." The resource server is the server that contains the user's information that is being accessed by the third-party application. The resource server must be able to accept and validate access tokens and grant the request if the user has allowed it. The resource server does not necessarily need to know about applications.

The Authorization Server

The authorization server is what the user interacts with when an application is requesting access to their account. This is the server that displays the OAuth prompt, and where the user approves or denies the application's request. The authorization server is also responsible for granting access tokens after the user authorizes the application.

The Client

The client is the app that is attempting to act on the user's behalf or access the user's resources. Before the client can access the user's account, it needs to obtain permission. The client will obtain permission by either directing the user to the authorization server, or by asserting permission directly with the authorization server without interaction by the user.

Confidential Clients

Confidential clients are clients which have the ability to maintain the confidentiality of the `client_secret`. Typically these clients are only applications that run on a server under the control of the developer, where the source code is not accessible to users. These types of applications are commonly referred to as "web apps," since they are most often running on a web server.

Public Clients

Public clients cannot maintain the confidentiality of a client_secret, so the secret is not used for these apps. Both mobile apps and JavaScript apps are considered public clients. Since anyone running a JavaScript app can easily view the source code of the application, a secret would be visible there trivially. With mobile applications, the binary can be decompiled to extract strings. Any time the application is running on a device under the user's control, it should be considered a public client.

Access Token

An access token is the string used when making authenticated requests to the API. The string itself has no meaning to the application using it, but represents that the user has authorized a third-party application to access their account. The token has a corresponding duration of access, scope, and potentially other information the server needs.

Refresh Token

A refresh token is a string that is used to get a new access token when an access token expires. Not all APIs use refresh tokens.

Authorization Code

An authorization code is an intermediate token used in the authorization code flow, described in more detail in Chapter 4, *Server-Side Apps*. An authorization code is returned to the client after the authorization step, and then the client exchanges it for an access token.

Chapter 21
Differences Between OAuth 1 and 2

OAuth 2.0 is a complete rewrite of OAuth 1.0 from the ground up, sharing only overall goals and general user experience. OAuth 2.0 is not backwards compatible with OAuth 1.0 or 1.1, and should be thought of as a completely new protocol.

OAuth 1 is considered deprecated, as it had many shortcomings when it started being applied to the modern web and client-side and native applications.

OAuth 1.0 was largely based on two existing proprietary APIs: Flickr and Google. The work that became OAuth 1.0 was the best solution based on actual implementation experience at the time. Over a few years of many companies building OAuth 1 APIs, and many developers writing code to consume the APIs, the community learned where the protocol was proving challenging. Several specific areas were identified as needing improvement because they were either limiting the abilities of the APIs, or were too challenging to implement.

OAuth 2.0 represents years of discussions between a wide range of companies and individuals including Yahoo!, Facebook, Salesforce, Microsoft, Twitter, Deutsche Telekom, Intuit, Mozilla and Google.

This section covers the major differences between OAuth 1.0 and 2.0, and the motivations behind them. If you are familiar with OAuth 1.0, this is a good starting point to quickly understand the major changes in OAuth 2.0.

Terminology and Roles

Where OAuth 2.0 defines four roles, (client, authorization server, resource server, and resource owner,) OAuth 1 uses a different set of terms for these roles. The OAuth 2.0 "client" is known as the "consumer," the "resource owner" is known simply as the "user," and the "resource server" is known as the "service provider". OAuth 1 also does not explicitly separate the roles of resource server and authorization server.

The terms "two-legged" and "three-legged" have been replaced by the idea of grant types, such as the Client Credentials grant type (page 132) and the Authorization Code grant type (page 128).

Authentication and Signatures

The majority of failed OAuth 1.0 implementation attempts were unsuccessful due to the cryptographic requirements of the protocol. The complexity of OAuth 1.0 signatures was a major pain point for anyone coming from the simplicity of username/password authentication.

Developers used to be able to quickly write Twitter scripts to do useful things by using just their username and password. With the move to OAuth 1.0, these developers were forced to find, install, and configure libraries in order to make requests to the Twitter API since it requires cryptographic signing of each request.

With the introduction of OAuth 2.0 Bearer tokens, it is again possible to quickly make API calls from a cURL command. The access token is used instead of a username and password.

For example, before OAuth, you may have seen examples in API docs such as:

```
curl --user bob:pa55 https://api.example.com/profile
```

With OAuth 1 APIs, it become no longer possible to hard-code an example like this, since the request must be signed with the application's secret. Some services such as Twitter started providing "signature generator" tools in their developer websites so that you could generate a curl command from the website without using a library. For example, the tool on Twitter generates a curl command such as:

```
curl --get 'https://api.twitter.com/1.1/statuses/show.json' \
--data 'id=210462857140252672' \
--header 'Authorization: OAuth oauth_consumer_key="xRhHSKcKLl9VF7",
oauth_nonce="33ec5af28add281c63db55d1839d90f1",
oauth_signature="oBO19fJO8imCAMvRxmQJsA6idXk%3D",
oauth_signature_method="HMAC-SHA1",
oauth_timestamp="1471026075",
oauth_token="12341234-ZgJYZOh5Z3ldYXH2sm5voEs0pPXOPv8vC0mFjMFtG",
oauth_version="1.0"'
```

With OAuth 2.0 Bearer Tokens, only the token itself is needed in the request, so the examples again become very simple:

```
curl https://api.example.com/profile \
-H "Authorization: Bearer XXXXXXXXXXX"
```

This provides a good balance between ease of use of APIs and good security practices.

User Experience and Alternative Token Issuance Options

There are two main parts to OAuth 2.0: obtaining authorization by the user (the end result being the application has an access token for that user), and using the access token to make requests on behalf of the user. The methods for obtaining an access token are called flows.

OAuth 1.0 started out with 3 flows, for web-based applications, desktop clients, and mobile or "limited" devices. However, as the specification evolved, the three flows were merged into one which, in theory, enabled all three client types. In practice, the flow worked fine for web-based applications but provided an inferior experience elsewhere.

As more sites started using OAuth, especially Twitter, developers realized that the single flow offered by OAuth was very limited and often produced poor user experiences. On the other hand, Facebook Connect offered a richer set of flows suitable for web applications, mobile devices, and game consoles.

OAuth 2.0 addresses this by defining multiple flows again, called "grant types," with flexibility to support a wide range of application types. There is also a mechanism to develop extensions to handle use cases not previously thought of.

Server-side apps use the "Authorization Code" grant type with a client secret, which prompts the user to authorize the application, and generates an authorization code that is handed back to the app. The app's server then exchanges the authorization code for an access token. The security of this flow is obtained by the fact that the server-side app uses its secret to exchange the authorization code for an access token.

Single-page or mobile apps use the same grant type, but don't use the client secret. Instead, the security is in verifying the redirect URL as well as the optional PKCE extension.

OAuth 2.0 officially defines a "Password" grant type, allowing applications to collect the user's username and password and exchange them for an access token. While this is part of the spec, it is intended to only be used by trusted clients, such as a service's own first-party application. It should not be used by third-party apps as that would allow the third-party app to have access to the username and password of the user.

The "Client Credentials" grant is used when an application is access its own resources. This grant type is simply exchanging the `client_id` and `client_secret` for an access token.

OAuth 2.0 also supports extension grant types allowing organizations to define their own custom grant types to support additional client types or to provide a bridge between OAuth and existing systems.

One such extension is the Device Flow (page 165) for authorizing apps on devices that don't have a web browser.

Performance at Scale

As larger providers started using OAuth 1.0, the community realized that the protocol had several limitations that made it difficult to scale to large systems. OAuth 1.0 requires state management across different steps and often across different servers. It requires generating temporary credentials which are often discarded unused, and typically requires issuing long lasting credentials which are less secure and harder to manage.

In addition, OAuth 1.0 requires that the protected resources endpoints have access to the client credentials in order to validate the request. This breaks the typical architecture of most large providers in which a centralized authorization server is used for issuing credentials, and a separate server is used for handling API calls. Because OAuth 1.0 requires the use of the client credentials to verify the signatures, it makes this separation very hard.

OAuth 2.0 addresses this by using the client credentials only when the application obtains authorization from the user. After the credentials are used in the authorization step, only the resulting access token is used when making API calls. This means the API servers do not need to know about the client credentials since they can validate access tokens themselves.

Bearer Tokens

In OAuth 1, there are two components to the access token, a public and private string. The private string is used when signing the request, and never sent across the wire.

The most common way of accessing OAuth 2.0 APIs is using a "Bearer Token". This is a single string which acts as the authentication of the API request, sent in an HTTP "Authorization" header. The string is meaningless to clients using it, and may be of varying lengths.

Bearer tokens are a much simpler way of making API requests, since they don't require cryptographic signing of each request. The tradeoff is that all API requests must be made over an HTTPS connection, since the request contains a plaintext token that could be used by anyone if it were intercepted. The advantage is that it doesn't require complex libraries to make requests and is much simpler for both clients and servers to implement.

The downside to Bearer tokens is that there is nothing preventing other apps from using a Bearer token if it can get access to it. This is a common criticism of OAuth 2.0, although most providers only use Bearer tokens anyway. Under normal circumstances, when applications properly protect the access tokens under their control, this is not a problem, although technically it is less secure. If your service requires a more secure approach, you can a different access token type that may meet your security requirements.

Short-Lived Tokens with Long-Lived Authorizations

OAuth 1.0 APIs typically issued extremely long-lasting access tokens. These tokens could last indefinitely, or on the order of a year. While convenient for developers, this proved limiting to some service providers in certain situations.

Responsible API providers should allow users to see which third-party apps they have authorized to use their account, and should be able to revoke apps if desired. If a user revokes an app, the API should stop accepting the access tokens issued to that app as soon as possible. Depending on how the API was implemented, this could be challenging or require additional ties between internal parts of the system.

With OAuth 2.0, the authorization server can issue a short-lived access token and a long-lived refresh token. This allows apps to obtain new access tokens without involving the user again, but also adds the ability for servers to revoke tokens easier. This feature was adopted from Yahoo!'s BBAuth protocol and later its OAuth 1.0 Session Extension.

See Refreshing Access Tokens on page 145 for more information.

Separation of Roles

One of the design decisions that went into OAuth 2.0 was to explicitly separate the roles of the authorization server from the API server. This means you can build out the authorization server as a standalone component which is only responsible for obtaining authorization from users and issuing tokens to clients. The two roles can be on physically separate servers, and even be on different domain names, allowing each part of the system to be scaled independently. Some providers have many resource servers and each is on a different subdomain.

The authorization server needs to know about the app's `client_id` and `client_secret`, but the API server will only ever need to accept access tokens. By building the authorization server as a standalone component, you can avoid sharing a database with the API servers, making it easier to scale API servers independently of the authorization server since they don't need to share a common data store.

For example, Google's OAuth 2.0 implementation uses a server at "accounts.google.com" for authorization requests, but uses "www.gooogleapis.com" when making requests to the Google+ API.

The benefit to service providers is that the development of these systems can happen completely independently, by different teams and on different timelines. Since they are completely separate, they can be scaled independently, or upgraded or replaced without concerning the other parts of the systems.

Chapter 22
OpenID Connect

The OAuth 2.0 framework explicitly does not provide any information about the user that has authorized an application. OAuth 2.0 is a *delegation* framework, allowing third-party applications to act on behalf of a user, without the application needing to know the identity of the user.

OpenID Connect takes the OAuth 2.0 framework and adds an identity layer on top. It provides information about the user, as well as enables clients to establish login sessions. While this chapter is not meant to be a complete guide to OpenID Connect, it is meant to clarify how OAuth 2.0 and OpenID Connect relate to each other.

Authorization vs Authentication

OAuth 2.0 is called an authorization "framework" rather than a "protocol" since the core spec actually leaves quite a lot of room for various implementations to do things differently depending on their use cases. Specifically, OAuth 2.0 does not provide a mechanism to say who a user is or how they authenticated, it just says that a user delegated an application to act on their behalf. The OAuth 2.0 framework provides this delegation in the form of an access token, which the application can use to act on behalf of the user. The access token is presented to the API (the "resource server"), which knows how to validate whether the access token is active. From the application's perspective, it is an opaque string.

When you check in to a hotel, you get a key card which you can use to enter your assigned room. You can think of the key card as an access token. The key card says nothing about who you are, or how you were authenticated at the front desk, but you can use the card to access your hotel room for the duration of your stay. Similarly, an OAuth 2.0 access token doesn't indicate who a user is, it just is the thing you can use to access data, and it may expire at some point in the future.

OAuth 2.0 was intentionally designed to provide authorization without providing user identity and authentication, as those problems have very different security considerations that don't necessarily overlap with those of an authorization protocol. Treating authentication and identity separately allows the OAuth 2.0 framework to be used as part of building an authentication protocol.

Building an Authentication Framework

It is quite possible to use the OAuth 2.0 framework as the basis for building an authentication and identity protocol.

To use OAuth 2.0 as the basis of an authentication protocol, you will need to do at least a few things.

- Define an endpoint to return attributes about a user
- Define one or more scopes that the third-party applications can use to request identity information from the user
- Define additional error codes and the necessary extension parameters for the scenarios you'll encounter when dealing with authentication and identity, such as when to re-prompt for the user's credentials based on session timeouts, or how to allow the user to select a new account when signing in to an application

Typically when a single provider attempts to add things to OAuth 2.0 to create an authentication and identity protocol, this results in another snowflake API with varying degrees of security. OpenID

Connect takes the shared knowledge gained from many different implementations and standardizes it into a protocol suitable for enterprise grade implementations.

ID Tokens

The core of OpenID Connect is based on a concept called "ID Tokens." This is a new token type that the authorization server will return which encodes the user's authentication information. In contrast to access tokens, which are only intended to be understood by the resource server, ID tokens are intended to be understood by the OAuth client. When the client makes an OpenID Connect request, it can request an ID token along with an access token.

OpenID Connect's ID Tokens take the form of a JWT (JSON Web Token), which is a JSON payload that is signed with the private key of the issuer, and can be parsed and verified by the application.

Inside the JWT are a handful of defined property names that provide information to the application. They are represented with shorthand names to keep the overall size of the JWT small. This includes a unique identifier for the user (`sub`, short for "subject"), the identifier for the server that issued the token (`iss`), the identifier for the client that requested this token (`aud`, short for "audience"), along with a handful of properties such as the lifetime of the token, and how long ago the user was presented with a primary authentication prompt.

```
{
  "iss": "https://server.example.com",
  "sub": "24400320",
  "aud": "s6BhdRkqt3",
  "nonce": "n-0S6_WzA2Mj",
  "exp": 1311281970,
  "iat": 1311280970,
  "auth_time": 1311280969
}
```

Standardizing the endpoints, names, and metadata helps reduce implementation errors, and allows shared knowledge to be passed around about the security considerations of each.

Summary

OpenID Connect provides user identity and authentication on top of the OAuth 2.0 framework. You can use OpenID Connect to establish a login session, and use OAuth to access protected resources.

You can request both an ID token and access token in the same flow in order to both authenticate the user as well as obtain authorization to access a protected resource.

OpenID Connect is maintained by the OpenID Foundation *(https://openid.net)*. The core OpenID Connect spec, as well as many extensions, can be read in full on *https://openid.net/connect/*.

The OpenID Connect Debugger *(https://oidcdebugger.com/)* is a fantastic resource to help you build OpenID Connect requests and walk through the flows. Additionally, the OAuth 2.0 Playground *(https://www.oauth.com/playground/)* provides a walkthrough of the OpenID Connect flow against a live server.

In Chapter 3, *Signing in with Google*, we walk through building a sample app using OpenID Connect.

Chapter 23

IndieAuth

IndieAuth is a decentralized identity protocol built on OAuth 2.0, which works using URLs to identify users and applications. It allows people to use a website under their control as their identity while signing in and authorizing applications using that identity. The spec can be found at *https://www.w3.org/TR/indieauth/*.

All user IDs are URLs, and apps are also identified by their URLs instead of by pre-registered client IDs. This makes it work great for situations where you don't want to require that developers sign up for an account at each authorization server, such as writing apps that authenticate users at arbitrary WordPress installations.

IndieAuth can be used as an authentication mechanism when an application just needs to identify users for login, or it can be used by an application to obtain an access token to use against the user's website.

For example, IndieAuth is used by Micropub clients *(https://www.w3.org/TR/micropub/)* to obtain an access token that is then used to create content on the user's website.

IndieAuth builds upon the OAuth 2.0 framework as follows:

- Specifies a mechanism and format for identifying users (a resolvable URL)
- Specifies a method of discovering the authorization and token endpoints given a profile URL
- Specifies a format for the Client ID (also as resolvable URL)
- All clients are public clients, as client secrets are not used
- Client registration is not necessary, since all clients must use a resolvable URL as their Client ID
- Redirect URI registration is accomplished by either having a matching hostname for the redirect URI and client ID, or the application publicizing their valid redirect URLs on their website

More information and the spec can be found at *indieauth.net*. A brief overview of the two workflows follows.

Discovery

Before the app can redirect to the authorization server, the app needs to know *which* authorization server to direct the user to! This is because each user is identified by a URL, and the user's URL indicates where its authorization server lives.

The app first needs to prompt the user to enter their URL, or obtain their URL some other way. Typically apps will include a single URL field for the user to enter their URL.

The app will make an HTTP GET request to the user's profile URL, looking for either an HTTP `Link` header or an HTML `<link>` tag with a `rel` value of `authorization_endpoint`. In the case that the client is also trying to obtain an access token for the user, it will also look for a `rel` value of `token_endpoint`.

For example, a GET request to `https://aaronparecki.com/` may return the following, shown as an abbreviated HTTP request.

```
HTTP/2 200
content-type: text/html; charset=UTF-8
link: <https://aaronparecki.com/auth>; rel="authorization_endpoint"
link: <https://aaronparecki.com/token>; rel="token_endpoint"
link: <https://aaronparecki.com/micropub>; rel="micropub"

<!doctype html>
<meta charset="utf-8">
<title>Aaron Parecki</title>
<link rel="authorization_endpoint" href="/auth">
<link rel="token_endpoint" href="/token">
<link rel="micropub" href="/micropub">
...
```

Note that the endpoint URLs may be relative or absolute URLs, and may be on the same domain or on a different domain than the user's endpoint. This allows the user to use hosted services for any component.

More details on discovery can be found at *https://indieauth.spec.indieweb.org/#discovery-by-clients*.

Sign-In Flow

The basic flow for a user signing in to an application is as follows.

- The user enters their personal URL in the sign-in form of the application.
- **Discovery:** The application fetches the URL and finds the user's authorization endpoint.
- **Authorization Request:** The application directs the user's browser to the authorization endpoint discovered, as a standard OAuth 2.0 Authorization Grant along with the user's URL entered in the first step.
- **Authentication/Approval:** The user authenticates at their authorization endpoint and approves the login request. The authorization server generates an authorization code and redirects back to the application's redirect URL.
- **Verification:** The application checks the code at the authorization endpoint, similar to exchanging the code for

an access token, except no access token is returned since this is just a check for authentication. The authorization endpoint responds with the full URL of the user who authenticated.

Authentication Request

When the application builds the URL to authenticate the user, the request looks very similar to the OAuth authorization request with PKCE, except no pre-registration of the client is necessary, and the request may also include the user's profile URL. The URL will look like the below.

```
https://user.example.net/auth?
    response_type=code
    &me=https://user.example.net/
    &redirect_uri=https://example-app.com/redirect
    &client_id=https://example-app.com/
    &state=1234567890
    &code_challenge=XXXXXXXXX
    &code_challenge_method=S256
```

The authorization server will then ask the user to log in, as normally happens with OAuth flows, and then ask the user if they would like to continue signing into the app, as shown in Figure 23-1.

If the user approves, they will be redirected back to the application with an authorization code (and the app's state value) in the query string.

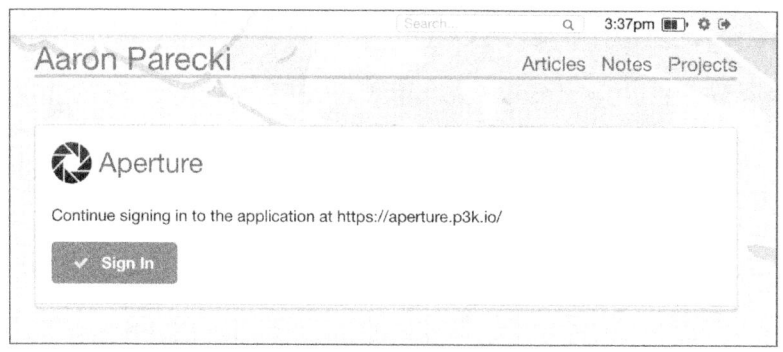

Figure 23-1: An IndieAuth login prompt

The app will then take the authorization code and verify it with the authorization endpoint, in order to confirm the identity of the user that signed in. The app makes a POST request to the authorization endpoint with the `code`, `client_id` and `redirect_uri`, like a typical authorization code exchange.

```
POST /auth
Host: user.example.net
Content-type: application/x-www-form-urlencoded

code=xxxxxxxx
&client_id=https://example-app.com/
&redirect_uri=https://example-app.com/redirect
&code_verifier=XXXXXXXXX
```

The response will be a simple JSON object with the user's full profile URL.

```
HTTP/1.1 200 OK
Content-Type: application/json

{
  "me": "https://user.example.net/"
}
```

See *https://indieauth.spec.indieweb.org/#redeeming-the-authorization-code* for more details about handling the request and response.

Authorization Flow

When an application is trying to obtain an access token for a user in order to modify or access a user's data, the authorization workflow is used instead. This is analogous to the OAuth 2.0 Authorization Code flow described in Chapter 2, except without pre-registration of clients since URLs are used instead.

The basic flow for a user authorizing an application follows:

- The user enters their personal URL in the sign-in form of the application.
- **Discovery:** The application fetches the URL and finds the user's authorization and token endpoints.
- **Authorization Request:** The application directs the user's browser to the authorization endpoint discovered, as a standard OAuth 2.0 Authorization Grant and requested scopes, along with the user's URL entered in the first step.
- **Authentication/Approval:** The user authenticates at their authorization endpoint, sees the requested scopes, and approves the request. The authorization server generates an authorization code and redirects back to the application's redirect URL.
- **Token Exchange:** The application makes a request to the token endpoint to exchange the authorization code for an access token. The token endpoint responds with an access token as well as the full URL of the user who authenticated.

Authorization Request

When the application builds the URL to authenticate the user, the request looks very similar to the OAuth authorization request, except no pre-registration of the client is necessary, and the request will also include the user's profile URL. The URL will look like the below.

```
https://user.example.net/auth?
    me=https://user.example.net/
    &response_type=code
    &redirect_uri=https://example-app.com/redirect
    &client_id=https://example-app.com/
    &state=1234567890
    &code_challenge=XXXXXXXXXXXXXXXX
    &code_challenge_method=S256
    &scope=create+update
```

Note that unlike in the authentication request above, this request includes a list of requested scopes the app is requesting.

The authorization server will ask the user to log in, then present them with an authorization prompt.

Different IndieAuth servers may present this prompt differently, as shown in the screenshots from my website's authorization server Figure 23-2 and the WordPress IndieAuth plugin in Figure 23-3.

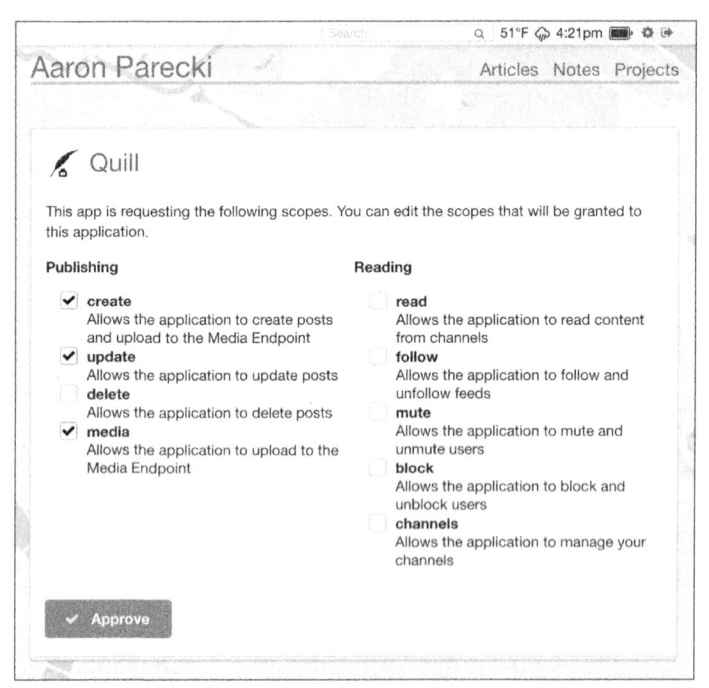

Figure 23-2: An IndieAuth authorization prompt on aaronparecki.com

When the user approves the request, the server redirects the user back to the application with an authorization code in the query string.

To obtain an access token, the application makes a POST request to the user's token endpoint (the endpoint was discovered in the first discovery step) with the authorization code and other required data.

```
POST /token
Host: user.example.net
Content-type: application/x-www-form-urlencoded

grant_type=authorization_code
&code=xxxxxxxx
&client_id=https://example-app.com/
&redirect_uri=https://example-app.com/redirect
&code_verifier=XXXXXXXXXXXXX
```

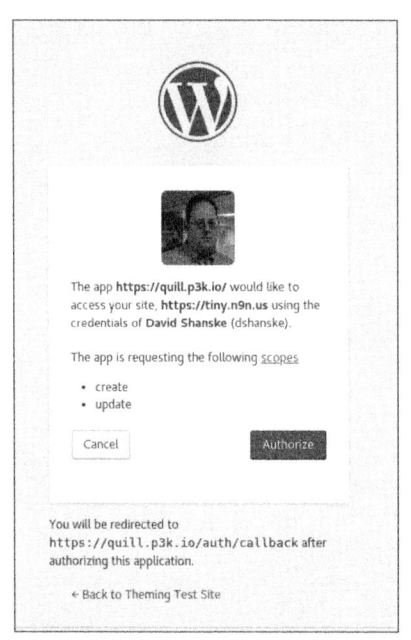

Figure 23-3: An authorization prompt from the WordPress IndieAuth Plugin

The token endpoint will generate an access token for the user, and respond with a normal OAuth 2.0 token response with the addition of the profile URL of the user who authorized the app.

```
HTTP/1.1 200 OK
Content-Type: application/json

{
  "me": "https://user.example.net/",
  "token_type": "Bearer",
  "access_token": "XXXXXX",
  "scope": "create update"
}
```

Chapter 24

Map of OAuth 2.0 Specs

The OAuth 2.0 Core Framework (RFC 6749) defines roles and a base level of functionality, but leaves a lot of implementation details unspecified. Since the publication of the RFC, the OAuth Working Group has published many additional specs built on top of this framework to fill in the missing pieces. Looking at the full list of specs *(https://tools.ietf.org/wg/oauth/)* the group is working on can be somewhat overwhelming. This chapter lays out how the various specs relate to each other.

Core Specs

OAuth 2.0 Core (RFC 6749)

https://datatracker.ietf.org/doc/html/rfc6749

RFC 6749 is the core OAuth 2.0 framework. This describes the roles (resource owner, client, authorization server, etc, described in more detail in Chapter 20, *Terminology Reference,*), several authorization flows, and several error definitions. It is important to remember that this is a "framework," as there are many aspects left unspecified that you'll need to fill out when building a complete implementation. Much of these details have been documented as extension specs.

Bearer Token Usage (RFC 6750)

https://datatracker.ietf.org/doc/html/rfc6750

Access token usage is defined in RFC 6750, although the format of access tokens isn't defined here. This spec defines "Bearer Tokens", which just means that it's a type of token that can be used by whoever has the token with no additional information. The particular format access tokens take (random strings, JWTs, etc) is not relevant to OAuth clients so isn't included in this spec. Only the Authorization Server and Resource Server need to coordinate on access token formats, so that is left up to the particular implementation or a future spec.

PKCE: Proof Key for Code Exchange (RFC 7636)

https://datatracker.ietf.org/doc/html/rfc7636

PKCE is an extension to the Authorization Code flow that adds a secure link between starting and completing the flow to prevent authorization codes from being used if intercepted.

PKCE works by the app first generating a new secret each time it starts the Authorization Code flow, and it sends a hash of the secret in the initial authorization request. The original secret is then required in order to exchange the authorization code for an access token, ensuring that even if an attacker can steal the authorization code, they would be unable to use it.

At the time of publication, PKCE was recommended for mobile apps, but it has proven to be useful even for JavaScript apps, and now the latest Security Best Current Practice recommends using it for all types of apps, even apps with a client secret.

Threat Model and Security Considerations (RFC 6819)

https://datatracker.ietf.org/doc/html/rfc6819

The Threat Model and Security Considerations document was written to provide additional guidance beyond what is described in the core RFC. Much of this document was added after major providers had real implementation experience. The document describes many known attacks, either theoretical attacks or ones that have been demonstrated in the wild. It describes countermeasures for each.

Everyone implementing an OAuth 2.0 server should read this document to avoid falling into traps that have already been explored and solved.

OAuth 2.0 Security Best Current Practice (Security BCP)

https://datatracker.ietf.org/doc/html/draft-ietf-oauth-security-topics

OAuth 2.0 Security Best Current Practice describes security requirements and other recommendations for clients and servers implementing OAuth 2.0. This is a new Best Current Practice around OAuth security, intended to capture experience gained from live deployments in the years since the first Security Considerations RFC was published in 2013.

This spec is also still in draft form, so will likely go through a few more changes before it is finalized as an RFC.

Some of the concrete recommendations in this draft are deprecating the Implicit flow and Password grant, and recommending that a new refresh token is issued every time one is used.

Tokens

Token Revocation (RFC 7009)

https://datatracker.ietf.org/doc/html/rfc7009

Token Revocation describes a new endpoint on the authorization server that clients can use to notify the server that an access token or refresh token is no longer needed. This is used to enable a "log out" feature in clients, allowing the authorization server to clean up any tokens or other data associated with that session.

Token Introspection (RFC 7662)

https://datatracker.ietf.org/doc/html/rfc7662

The Token Introspection spec defines a mechanism for resource servers to obtain information about access tokens. Without this spec, resource servers have to have a bespoke way of checking whether access tokens are valid, and finding out user data about them, etc. This typically occurs by either a custom API endpoint, or because the resource server and authorization server share a database or some other common storage.

With this spec, resource servers can check the validity of access tokens and find out other information with an HTTP API call, leading to better separation of concerns between the authorization server and any resource servers.

JWT Profile for OAuth Access Tokens (RFC 9068)

https://datatracker.ietf.org/doc/html/rfc9068

The JWT Profile defines a JWT-based format and vocabulary for access tokens based on the collective experience learned from several large deployments.

Mobile and Other Devices

These specs are written to enable support of OAuth on a wider variety of devices.

OAuth 2.0 for Native Apps (RFC 8252)

https://datatracker.ietf.org/doc/html/rfc8252

The intended audience for this spec is implementers of mobile apps or apps running on desktop devices, where interactions between the app and the browser are not as straightforward as in a browser-only environment.

In this document you'll find security recommendations unique to the native application environment. It describes things like not allowing the third-party application to open an embedded web view which is more susceptible to phishing attacks, as well as platform-specific recommendations on how to do so. It also recommends using the PKCE extension.

Browser-Based Apps

datatracker.ietf.org/doc/html/draft-ietf-oauth-browser-based-apps

OAuth 2.0 for Browser-Based Apps describes security requirements and other recommendations for JavaScript apps (commonly known as Single-Page Apps) using OAuth.

As of this publication, this document is still in draft form and is not yet an RFC. It is likely to go through some more changes before it is finalized. It has been adopted by the working group, which means people broadly recognize the need for this kind of guidance, although the specific recommendations inside have not necessarily yet been fully agreed upon yet.

This document is intended to complement the Native App Best Current Practice, addressing the specifics of a browser-based environment instead.

It recommends using the Authorization Code flow with PKCE instead of using the Implicit flow, and disallowing the Password grant by browser apps. It also provides a few different architectural patterns available to these apps.

Device Authorization Grant (RFC 8628)

https://datatracker.ietf.org/doc/html/rfc8628

The Device Authorization Grant is an extension that enables devices with no browser or limited input capability to use OAuth. You'll typically see this on devices like the Apple TV where there is no web browser, or streaming video encoders where there is no keyboard.

The flow works by having users visit a URL on a secondary device like a smartphone and entering a code that is shown on the device.

The Device Flow is described in more detail in Chapter 16, *OAuth for Browserless and Input-Constrained Devices*.

Authentication and Identification

These specs are used to provide applications with a user's identity, which is not provided by the core OAuth spec.

OpenID Connect

https://openid.net/connect/

Since the OAuth framework only describes an authorization method and does not provide any details about the user, OpenID Connect fills this gap by describing an authentication and session management mechanism.

We cover a brief overview of how OpenID Connect relates to OAuth 2.0 in Chapter 22, *OpenID Connect*.

IndieAuth

https://indieauth.spec.indieweb.org/

IndieAuth is a decentralized identity protocol built on OAuth 2.0, using URLs to identify users and applications. This avoids the need for prior registration of clients, since all clients have a built-in client ID: the application's URL.

We cover a brief overview of the authentication and authorization workflows of IndieAuth in Chapter 23, *IndieAuth*.

Interop

In order to support creating completely generic clients that can work with any OAuth 2.0 server, things such as discovery and client registration need to be standardized, since they are out of scope of the core spec.

Authorization Server Metadata (RFC 8414)

https://datatracker.ietf.org/doc/html/rfc8414

The Authorization Server Metadata spec (also known as Discovery) defines a format for clients to use to look up the information needed to interact with a particular OAuth server. This includes things like finding the authorization endpoint, and listing the supported scopes.

Dynamic Client Registration (RFC 7591)

https://datatracker.ietf.org/doc/html/rfc7591

Typically developers will manually register an application at a service to obtain a Client ID and provide information about the application that will be used on the authorization interface. This spec provides a mechanism for dynamically or programmatically registering clients. This spec was derived from the OpenID Connect Dynamic Client Registration spec and is still compatible with OpenID Connect servers.

Dynamic Client Management (RFC 7592)

https://datatracker.ietf.org/doc/html/rfc7592

In the case that client information needs to be updated, this spec provides a mechanism for doing so programmatically. This spec extends the Dynamic Registration RFC 7591, but is considered experimental still.

High Security

There are a few extensions to OAuth that provide higher levels of security compared to the base profile. Some of these are part of the Financial-Grade API work being done in OpenID Connect as well.

Pushed Authorization Requests (RFC 9126)

https://datatracker.ietf.org/doc/html/rfc9126

Pushed Authorization Requests is a significant change to the OAuth flow to rely less on the front channel, by moving the start of the authorization code flow to the back channel instead.

JWT Authorization Request (RFC 9101)

https://datatracker.ietf.org/doc/html/rfc9101

JWT Authorization Request describes a way to encode and sign the authorization request parameters as a JWT instead of using plain query string components. This lets the authorization server be sure that a particular OAuth application initiated the authorziation request and the request has not been forged or tampered with.

Mutual TLS Bound Access Tokens (RFC 8705)

https://datatracker.ietf.org/doc/html/rfc8705

Mutual TLS Certificate-Bound Access Tokens describes a way to use TLS certificates for client authentication as well as issuing certificate-bound access tokens. This is one way implementers are improving the security of bearer tokens.

Experimental Specs

These are early drafts of some new specs that may end up becoming part of OAuth 2.0. These specs enable additional use cases, or provide better security. These are all still early drafts, so they may change significantly by the time you're reading this, or may have been dropped entirely. These are some things to keep an eye on if you're interested in keeping up to date with the latest developments in the space.

Rich Authorization Requests

https://datatracker.ietf.org/doc/html/draft-ietf-oauth-rar

Rich Authorization Requests describes way for apps to request permissions more fine-grained than the current OAuth "scope" mechanism can provide. This could be used, for example, to authorize a particular bank transfer.

DPoP

https://datatracker.ietf.org/doc/html/draft-fett-oauth-dpop

DPoP describes an alternative to Mutual TLS for issuing access tokens that are bound to a particular client. This version accomplishes that in the application layer rather than transport layer.

Enterprise

These specs support more advanced enterprise use cases.

Assertion Framework (RFC 7521)

https://datatracker.ietf.org/doc/html/rfc7521

This spec provides a framework for using assertions with OAuth 2.0. It defines a new client authentication mechanism and a new authorization grant type. As this spec is also a framework, it is only useful with one of the specific assertion types described below.

JWT Profile for Client Authentication (RFC 7523)

https://datatracker.ietf.org/doc/html/rfc7523

This spec describes how a JWT can be used for client authentication in place of a client secret. This method is more secure than using a shared client secret as the private key never needs to leave the client, and is instead used to sign a JWT.

SAML Assertions (RFC 7522)

https://datatracker.ietf.org/doc/html/rfc7522

This spec describes how a SAML Assertion can be used to request an access token when there is an existing trust relationship with the client. This can be used, for example, to integrate legacy SAML workflows with new OAuth 2.0 systems.

○ ○ ○ ○ ○

Tools and Libraries

OAuth 2.0 Playground

https://www.oauth.com/playground/

Figure 24-1: oauth.com/playground

The OAuth 2.0 Playground walks you through the various OAuth flows by interacting with a real OAuth 2.0 authorization server.

It has examples of the Authorization Code flow, PKCE, the Device flow, as well as a simple example of OpenID Connect.

Example OAuth Client

https://example-app.com/client

This is an example OAuth client that you can configure using your own OAuth server's authorization endpoint and token endpoint, provide a client ID and optional secret, and step through the OAuth flow with the live server. The tool will show you each redirect or request before it's made so you can see the exact steps in the process.

OpenID Connect Debugger

https://oidcdebugger.com

The OpenID Connect Debugger allows you to test OpenID Connect requests and debug responses from the servers. You can configure the tool to work with any OpenID server such as Google's.

Directory of Server and Client Libraries

https://oauth.net/code/

The oauth.net website contains a directory of servers, clients and services that support OAuth 2.0. You can find anything from complete OAuth 2.0 server implementations to libraries that facilitate each step of the process, as well as client libraries and proxy services.

If you have any libraries or services to contribute, you can add them to the directory as well.

jwt.io

https://jwt.io/

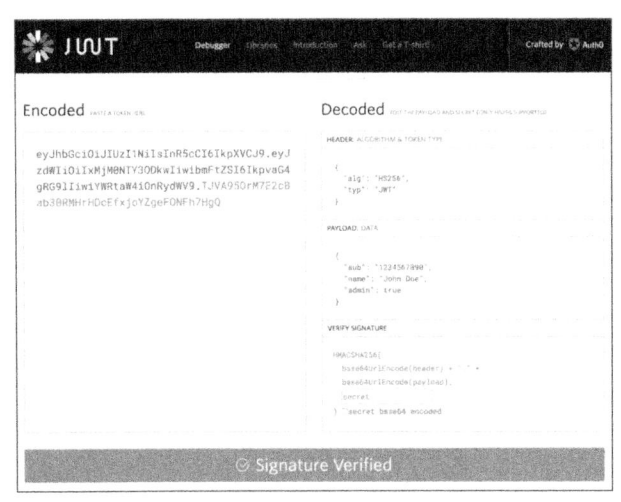

Figure 24-2: jwt.io

JWT.io (Figure 24-2) is a tool for debugging JSON Web Tokens. It allows you to paste a JWT and it will decode it and show the individual components. It can also verify the signature if you provide it with the secret that was used to sign the JWT.

Videos about OAuth

https://oauth.net/videos/

There is a great collection of videos about various OAuth topics at oauth.net/videos. Feel free to add yours as well by following the link at the bottom of the website!

References

Specifications

- OAuth 2.0 (RFC 6749)
  https://datatracker.ietf.org/doc/html/rfc6749
- Bearer Token Usage (RFC 6750)
  https://datatracker.ietf.org/doc/html/rfc6750
- OAuth 2.0 Threat Model and Security Considerations
  https://datatracker.ietf.org/doc/html/rfc6819
- Proof Key for Code Exchange (RFC 7636)
  https://datatracker.ietf.org/doc/html/rfc7636
- OAuth 2.0 for Native Apps
  https://datatracker.ietf.org/doc/html/rfc8252
- OAuth 2.0 Device Flow
  https://datatracker.ietf.org/doc/html/rfc8628
- JWT Profile for OAuth 2.0 Access Tokens
  https://datatracker.ietf.org/doc/html/rfc9068
- OAuth 2.0 Token Revocation
  https://datatracker.ietf.org/doc/html/rfc7009
- OpenID Connect
  https://openid.net/connect/
- IndieAuth
  https://indieauth.spec.indieweb.org/
- All OAuth Working Group Specs
  https://tools.ietf.org/wg/oauth/

Appendix: References

Vendor Documentation

- Google OAuth 2.0
  https://developers.google.com/identity/protocols/OAuth2
- Facebook Developers
  https://developers.facebook.com/
- GitHub Documentation
  https://developer.github.com/apps/
- Foursquare Documentation
  https://developer.foursquare.com/overview/auth
- FitBit Documentation
  https://dev.fitbit.com/build/reference/web-api/oauth2/

Community Resources

- OAuth articles by Aaron Parecki
  https://aaronparecki.com/articles?tag=oauth
- OAuth articles by Alex Bilbie
  https://alexbilbie.com/tag/oauth/
- User Authentication with OAuth 2.0
  https://oauth.net/articles/authentication/
- OAuth IETF Mailing List
  https://www.ietf.org/mailman/listinfo/oauth

About the Author

Aaron Parecki is a member of the OAuth Working Group at the IETF and has contributed to a number of the OAuth specifications. His books and trainings have helped thousands of developers build and architect secure systems using the latest standards.

He is also the co-founder of IndieWebCamp, a yearly worldwide conference on data ownership and online identity. He has spoken at conferences around the world about OAuth, data ownership, quantified self, and even explained why R is a vowel.

Aaron has tracked his location continuously since 2008, and was the co-founder and CTO of Geoloqi, a location-based software company acquired by Esri in 2012. His work has been featured in Wired, Fast Company and more, and made Inc. Magazine's 30 Under 30 for his work on Geoloqi. Aaron holds a B.S. in Computer Science from University of Oregon and lives in Portland, Oregon.

You can find Aaron at *aaronparecki.com* and *twitter.com/aaronpk*.

Printed in Great Britain
by Amazon